POMEGRANATES
AND GRAPES

Also by Nuray Aykın

Nuray Aykın edited professional books on usability and internationalization. Her work includes:

Usability and Internationalization of Information Technology
Usability and Internationalization: Global and Local User Interfaces
Usability and Internationalization: HCI and Culture
Internationalization, Design and Global Development

POMEGRANATES AND GRAPES

Landscapes from My Childhood

NURAY AYKIN

iUniverse, Inc.
Bloomington

Pomegranates and Grapes
Landscapes from My Childhood

iUniverse books may be ordered through booksellers or by contacting:

iUniverse
1663 Liberty Drive
Bloomington, IN 47403
www.iuniverse.com
1-800-Authors (1-800-288-4677)

Because of the dynamic nature of the Internet, any web addresses or links contained in this book may have changed since publication and may no longer be valid. The views expressed in this work are solely those of the author and do not necessarily reflect the views of the publisher, and the publisher hereby disclaims any responsibility for them.

Any people depicted in stock imagery provided by Thinkstock are models, and such images are being used for illustrative purposes only.
Certain stock imagery © Thinkstock.

ISBN: 978-1-4697-8747-3 (sc)
ISBN: 978-1-4697-8748-0 (hc)
ISBN: 978-1-4697-8749-7 (ebk)

Library of Congress Control Number: 2012903408

Printed in the United States of America

iUniverse rev. date: 03/21/2012

To Bora

and

to Al,

for being with me.

CONTENTS

Preface: Avlu to My Life xiii

1. Two Babies Born Thirty Years Apart.................................1
2. Where My Genes Come From: My Family.............................13
3. Places of My Childhood 42
4. Early School Years 69
5. College Years 75
6. I Married Your Dad..77
7. Off to Buffalo..81
8. My Teaching Years...100
9. Moving to New Jersey 108
10. AT&T Years and Beyond..114
11. I Found Love...116
12. When a Person Becomes a Parent 127

Afterword: Goodbye and Hello 129

"My head is bursting with the joy of the unknown.
My heart is expanding a thousand fold.
Every cell, taking wings, flies about the world.
All seek separately the many faces of my love."

Jelaluddin Rumi (1207-1273)

Acknowledgments

With deep heartfelt thanks to:

Pam Burke for giving me my first review and encouraging me to publish this book.

Luisa Farina for lending me her wonderful photograph as a book cover. She took it when we were on a Blue Voyage together on the Mediterranean.

Luisa Farina, Nora Sanburn, and Allen Milewski for sending me the most upbeat text messages to publish the book, for going an extra step and editing the manuscript.

Marie Dumbra for spending hours with me editing the final version of this book.

Gail Gold for giving me the sweetest feedback with her lovely hand-written notes.

Theresa and Vinny Kyne and Beth Bartley for telling me how much they loved the earlier versions of this book.

My family, especially my mom and Kara Dede, for showing me the beauty of this world and enjoying it no matter what.

Al for coming into my life at an unexpected time and making me a very happy woman. Without you, I would not be who I am.

And Bora for bringing me the joy and the challenges of raising a son.

PREFACE

Avlu to My Life

This is a book of my life, an *avlu,* a greeting/entrance area, to my life house. With this book, I will give you a tour of my *avlu,* entrance to my life, and then let you into my life house.

I told you many of my life stories during the last eighteen years we have been together. This book is a gift to you on your way to college. It is the story of my life, of me, what makes me Nuray Aykın: a mom, a business woman, a gardener, a wife, an ex-wife, a wife again, a daughter, a sister, an aunt, a stepmother, and maybe in the future, a grandmother.

I am not a writer, and this might be the only long story I will ever write. But it is a good story to tell, with ups and downs, laughter and tears, travels from east to west and north to south, changing seasons, different houses, different schools, different cars, different food, and different friends, each filled with stories to tell.

I am not perfect and will never be. I am me. I am a woman who started as a little girl in Tarsus, Turkey and moved to a big city, Ankara, and then moved to a different continent, North America. I traveled to many places and loved them all, for I love people and the places they live in and the cultures they reflect. I love to work, and I work to earn money to enjoy life. I love listening to the gentle laps of the azure blue Mediterranean Sea hitting the sparkling sandy beaches or smooth white pebbles. I love putting my face into the spring blossoms to inhale the new season. I love cooking for an army of friends during holidays, dancing around the house, flying to exotic places, hugging my mom, feeling the great pleasure of being your mom, and having a glass of wine with my dear husband Al. I love putting Christmas lights on, and watching our dog, Tornado, hugging me and inhaling my smell when I come home at night. I love sleeping in my bed, waking up before the sun is up, and calling my family in Turkey every weekend. I love just about everything. I can even tolerate winter as long as I have a book next to our fireplace with my grandfather's blanket of twenty-five plus years on my lap.

I hope you live your life to the fullest as I still do; there is nothing better than being alive and loving everything. Never stop *loving* people, all living things, and all places. Never stop *listening* to people, all living things, and all places. Be who you are, and know who you are. Believe in yourself that you will continue to stand on your feet no matter what happens around you. Then, you will be fine.

1

Two Babies Born Thirty Years Apart

My Birth

Our life journeys—yours and mine—took off from totally different starting points. My parents were poor when they got married. My father was a young high school mathematics teacher with a small teaching salary, and my mother was a housewife. They had my sister three years before I was born. My brother followed my sister in less than two years. My brother was only five months old when my mother was pregnant again. That was me in her, a little seedling becoming a person. They were barely making ends meet and thought it would be hard to feed three babies. They decided to end this pregnancy. They did not tell my grandmother (my father's mother). In Turkey we call her *babaanne*.

As you know, in Turkey there are different names for grandmothers: *Babaanne* for the father's mother, and *anneanne* for the mother's mother. From this you can easily deduce that *baba* means "father" and *anne* means "mother." Grandfathers are called the same on both sides: *dede*. In the past, the role of Turkish women, especially the mothers-in-law, was much stronger than that of men. *Babaanne* was more of an authority figure, and *anneanne* was more nurturing. Today, the roles they take depend on the personality of these grandmothers. Then, there is *hala* (father's sister) and *teyze* (mother's sister). *Teyze* is also used to address elderly women. When the younger generation starts calling a woman *teyze*, then it is time to start feeling depressed about being old. We call father's brother *amca*, mother's brother *Dayı*. Then there are *abi* (older brother), *abla* (older sister), *enişte* (sister's husband), *bacanak* (the name the husbands of sisters call each other), *baldız* (wife's sister), *elti* (the name the wives of brothers call each other), *görümce* (husband's sister), and so on. *Kuzen* is cousin, probably adapted from the French. I don't know why we have all these different names for all the relatives we have, but one thing is clear, family means a lot in Turkey. And, God forbid, you do not call your father-in-law by his first name.

There is an amazing social structure in the families. Everyone cares about one another no matter what his or her age is. Parents take care of their children until children take care of their parents. They visit each other very often with no agenda, just for love and a sense of belonging. If one needs money, or just a hug, the others are always ready to give it to them. This may cause a lot of poking into your relatives' lives, but believe me, it is worth it. They usually do not visit you just in your *avlu*. They do not stop there. They pass through the *avlu* pretty quickly to enter your house, sometimes without permission. You really do not have much privacy unless you cut your ties with the family. However, I would rather have my life be scrutinized by my family, who loves me with no strings attached, than be all alone in my life house with people in my *avlu* who do not care about me as much as my family does.

To continue my birth story, my parents went to the doctor for an abortion and found out that the doctor was gone for a family emergency. So they came home sheepishly, very worried, and did not know what to do. Their faces gave them away immediately. My grandmother, a very smart Anatolian woman who never went to school and never learned to read and write, guessed what was up. She told them, "If you do this, I will never forgive you. If you do not want this baby, then give it to me. I will raise it myself. I will share my food. I will wrap her with scrap fabrics. And we will make it somehow."

My parents knew then that what they were planning to do was not meant to be. I was spared. Several months later a little baby girl was born in a small apartment in Tarsus, a famous biblical city. Don't think that being unwanted affected me in any way. Nope! I was just a little girl who received tons of love, especially from my mom, my grandparents, and my siblings.

My parents never made me feel any different than my brother and sister. And, since I was the youngest, I could get away with a lot of mischief that my brother and my sister could not. My parents knew that I knew how much they loved me, and that made them very comfortable telling me my birth story.

Your Birth

Twenty-seven years later, I was ready to have children. I was married for four years and just completed my graduate studies. I love kids and I wanted to have at least three, just like my parents. Guess what! I could not have a baby that easily! All those years of birth control were meaningless. Apparently, there was no need for it.

Then came tests, surgeries, hormone therapy, and sadness. Every month, when I realized I was not pregnant (again and again), I cried. Three years passed. Then the summer of 1987 came, the summer of the Chernobyl nuclear accident. I was planning to go to Turkey. I was all excited, saying to myself, "This is great that I am not pregnant. I will enjoy my time in Turkey and come back and try again." Your dad left for Turkey before I did. I had to go to a conference to present a paper and had some work to finish at the university where I was teaching. A visiting professor from Turkey was staying with me. I flew to Washington, D.C. for my conference. During that time I was expecting my period and praying it would come late so that I would not have the cramps during my presentation. I am sure one day you will understand and give extra attention to your girlfriend or your wife. All women who have heavy painful periods know what I am talking about. So I was really happy that my period was delayed. I even had a beer at the hotel lobby after my presentation. A typical conference scene: a young professor, trying to act cool, feeling bored to death, not knowing anybody, all alone, and wishing to be home.

Well, I flew back home the next day. I realized maybe my period was not just delayed. I had butterflies in my stomach thinking I might be pregnant. There was that little hope, that "what if" hope. I kept telling myself not to get too excited so that I would not be disappointed again. The minute I arrived home I went to the only drugstore in Hornell, New York, ten miles from Alfred University, where I was teaching. I bought a home pregnancy test kit. The five-minute drive from the drug store to my home was my "hope drive." I kept hoping but, at the same time, tried to push away the idea. I was praying, begging, promising all kinds of things until I picked up the stick. Voila! Whatever color the test stick was supposed to turn to show that "you are pregnant" happened!

With the stick in my hand, I called my doctor, Teresita Gungon in Dansville, New York. I used to go to a gynecologist in Hornell but had bad experiences with her. I kept searching for a better doctor and finally found one in Dansville, about a forty-five-minute drive from Hornell. Dr. Gungon was one of the best doctors I ever had. She was from the Philippines, a beautiful, slim, mother of four girls, and always dressed in chic New Yorker clothes, even in the little town of Dansville. That evening, although the office was about to close, the nurse, knowing how crazy I was to get pregnant, asked me if I could make it in an hour. She promised that she would wait to get a blood test done and I could get the results the next morning. There was no way I could have missed that. I hopped in my old dark maroon Chevrolet Caprice Classic, a gasoline eater, with a hole between the driver's seat and the pedals. The hole was covered with just the carpeting. It ran really well that evening, and I made it to the doctor's office in time.

They called me early the next morning. It was true. I was pregnant! I was the happiest person in the world. However, I could not share my joy with anybody. My entire family, who would celebrate with me to the fullest, was not with me. That was one of those moments I really felt being away from my family. I spent the next few days spending a fortune on international phone calls, talking to your dad, who was still in Turkey, and my parents, my brother, and my sister. This is the moment one knows that being close to family really matters. I could not hug them, I could not dance around with them, I could not talk for hours, and I could not shop for baby clothes with them. You cannot share such joy from thousands of miles away. I wanted my mom and my sister with me, talking and shopping and dreaming together. I wanted to say "eee!" to little onesies. Instead your dad and I went to Sears, the only department store in Hornell besides K-Mart, just buying the basics, and leaving the store with the baby essentials—a crib, sheets, diapers, and some basic clothing. It was not at all an amazing experience.

Of course, I could not go to Turkey that summer. Chernobyl was very close to Turkey, and the radiation was definitely affecting the crops in the Black Sea region. I did not want to risk anything. I was glad I did not. A year later, the babies born in the Northern region of Turkey had deformities.

I decided to be a very healthy pregnant woman, especially after feeling very guilty about having one beer at the conference. I checked all the books about alcohol effects on a baby, and I could not find what the effect of a single beer would be. There was no internet then. My information sources were the book store about an hour away and the library at the university. I read everything I found about pregnancy. I ate right. I walked a lot. I mean *a lot*. You know how much I love walking. I walked at least an hour a day, rain or shine, hot or cold. Well, not really in the cold. You know I have a very low tolerance for cold. So, walking outdoors in upstate New York in winter was not something I could handle.

When the fall came, I was about four or five months pregnant. We moved to a bigger house in September so that we would have more space. It was a very beautiful old house, nestled in the woods, surrounded with blackberry bushes. The landlady left me bags of blackberries in the freezer. That is probably why you love berries so much. There was even a swimming pool. But unfortunately, we did not have a chance to put our feet in it.

I kept walking in the house every evening, forty minutes exactly, around the big stone fireplace right in the middle of the living room. I probably dug a groove in the carpet. While walking I could read, get ready for my next day's lecture, discuss research papers with your dad, or simply listen to the music and dance around.

You kept growing. And your dad kept putting more wood in the fireplace. Boy, you cannot imagine the amount of snow that falls and how cold it gets in upstate New York. I would go to bed in thick flannel pajamas and a big sweater. By the way, I still have those pajamas. I cannot throw things away until they really fall apart. Did I mention that I still have my grandfather's gift, my very soft blanket, which he gave to me when I was twenty-two? I still have the sweater that my mom bought me for my seventeenth birthday. She saved the money for my sweater by putting a few liras away here and there for six months. My dad was not at all a gift-giver. He did not even buy us things that we really needed. My mom had to do it secretly.

With all these preparations going on for your arrival, your dad and I were searching for jobs. We wanted to leave Alfred University, a small private university in upstate New York. We wanted to try our chances somewhere else. At Alfred, we were part of a very small department, showing all the signs of dying. So, we kept sending our resumes everywhere, mostly for teaching jobs. And we applied together. That did not work very well. We also sent individual resumes. Finally, I received a call from George Washington University. It was amazing. I felt so proud of myself, thinking "this is really a move up." I was probably one of the few women who went to a job interview eight months pregnant. It was an opportunity not to be missed. I had the interview in my one and only decent maternity dress that my sister sent me that summer. Well, it passed as a fancy silk dress on a dead-cold winter day when I put a coat over it. In December 1987, although I froze my bum, I did well during the interview. A few days later they offered me an Associate Professor position in the engineering management department starting the following academic year. I accepted the offer, put it aside, and went back to dealing with my pregnancy again. I was teaching two courses that fall at Alfred. Many days I would come home and rest a while before going back to my office. I would take a nap on a recliner chair with an apple on my tummy. I would watch the snow on the trees and the squirrels outside. Sometimes a deer or two would wander around. The house had big windows, and there was a huge jade tree by the window. Looking at the bright green leaves with snow in the background was very soothing. I still remember the image.

Speaking of maternity clothes, I kind of knew this was my only pregnancy and I would not be in need of any of them again. I managed the entire nine months with two dresses, two pairs of jeans, one pair of wool pants, and a couple of large sweaters.

Then the unforgettable morning came. It actually signaled its coming the day before. I literally scrubbed everything in the house: bathroom, toilets, kitchen, floor, everything. That was a real hormone rush. And that night, or actually four in the morning, I heard this whoosh sound in my belly, and then came the water. I did not know I could hold that much water in my tummy. In the bathroom sitting on the toilet, I kept hoping that the water rush would stop and then I would call the doctor. Nope. It kept coming. I woke your dad up and asked him to bring the telephone to me, still sitting on the toilet. My doctor told me to go to the hospital right away. That was scary. It was really scary, not just being very close to having a baby, but also going out on a dark, cold winter night, with ice everywhere. It was minus eighteen degrees. I baby-walked to the car, with a garbage bag between my legs, freezing, water running down my legs, and several plastic bags in my hand to put on the car seat. I kept leaking all the way to the hospital on our forty-five-minute ride. I walked to the emergency entrance with a large black garbage bag hanging between my legs. I was scared to death that I might fall on the ice.

The gynecologist on duty was not Dr. Gungon, but her partner. I really wanted Dr. Gungon to deliver you. Maybe that is why you and

I waited until Dr. Gungon took her turn at six o'clock that night. All those pregnant women came and went, one after another. I watched them get wheeled into the delivery room. There were screamers, cursers, happy ones, tired ones, skinny ones, fat ones, young ones, and old ones. They were all becoming mothers. They were all bringing their babies into this world. And imagine, all these babies have the same birthday you do.

We, the pregnant women at the hospital, had one thing in common: pain. And lots of it. It really gets you. I did not take Lamaze classes since the closest center offering them was at least thirty minutes away and I did not want to leave the warm fireplace to go to Lamaze classes in the cold. I pretended I knew all about it from what I learned from watching a Lamaze tape just once. I imagined the beautiful waves in Hawaii when we went to a conference there, when you were only a couple of months in my tummy.

I remember the day before our flight to Hawaii I got all the blood tests and amniocentesis done. That was the day I learned that I would have a baby boy. The doctor told me during the ultrasound that he saw a third leg. I still have the picture from the ultrasound, showing one of your hands on top of your head, as if you were pulling your hair with frustration. That is the same position you had when the nurse brought you next to me. Your first passport picture when you were forty days old had the same composition.

While imagining riding the waves in Hawaii, my pain was becoming unbearable. I decided not to scream. The chart next to me was showing really high peaks and they were out of range. Hurricane forces on my Hawaiian waves? When Dr. Gungon saw the charts, and knowing that I was still hours away from full dilation, she decided I could not continue this way. She ordered an epidural and soon I was deeply asleep but still feeling a push in my lower abdomen. It was about eight at night when I woke up with the feeling that I could not hold on any longer. I saw that they were monitoring your heart rate, and it was way below normal. Thanks to all the books I had read, I called the nurse immediately. She told me that I should not worry and that it is perfectly alright for a baby's heart rate to fluctuate. Me, worry? Sure. My baby's heart was not fluctuating, it was going down. I started screaming at her that she should get Dr. Gungon right away. Of course, Dr. Gungon heard the commotion and saw the chart. She knew there was no time left to wait for a natural childbirth.

Then, just like in the movies, they wheeled me out of the waiting area that I had been in for about fourteen hours. And with the nurses and my doctor pushing my bed at a high speed, with my doctor yelling orders, and also scolding the nurse, we were finally in the operating room. Since the lower part of my body was still numb, they quickly went ahead with a Caesarean section. The anesthesiologist gave me more anesthesia before the effect of the epidural ran out. He was telling me about the great food at a dinner party he had been at, and wished that I could have held out a little longer so that he could have had his dessert. He was a very sweet person. I watched in the tiny mirrors of the big operating room lights and saw how they pulled you out.

I watched a nurse lift you up and wrap you in a blanket. She put a cap on your head, a little cotton cap. It wasn't even a cap; it looked like a cotton tube tied in one end with a knot to make it a hat. The nurse brought you near my face so I could see you. She said the simplest and the most meaningful words, "Here is mommy." It is the moment you feel things are different. There is this little thing to take care of. That part is scary! This little thing that is so cute. That part is wonderful. You had soft, light honey-colored hair. And what big eyes! Big hazel eyes! Big questioning eyes. Your right hand was grabbing your hair. I held you a bit in my arms in that brightly lit operating room. And they whizzed you away to do some tests and also to show you to your dad. Your dad told me that you were quite heavy and his arms were hurting just holding you for a few long minutes. You were 8 pounds, 8 ounces, 18 inches long. You were born in 1988 at 8:32 p.m. A lot of eights! In the Chinese culture, the number eight means prosperity and wealth. The three eights together mean triple prosperity! I hope so.

Like any mother would say, you were the most beautiful baby for me, a handsome little boy. You still are. That is how you were born, my dear kiddo.

Our First Few Months

That night at the hospital was not at all enjoyable. The nurses kept giving me painkillers. Just my luck, I shared the room with a lady who had a natural, easy birth, maybe her second or third. She snored heavily all night long. I could not sleep. I kept calling the nurses and asking them to find a way to stop her snoring. There was no other room that they could move me to. So the nurses found a way to stop the snoring by waking my roommate up every twenty minutes to check her blood pressure. I had a few hours sleep. That is when my sleepless nights for the next few years began.

I stayed in the hospital for six days. That was not even close enough to recover from a Caesarean section. I needed at least another ten days, maybe even weeks or years. I was scared to go home with just you and your dad. My incision was still hurting a lot, with big staples on my tummy. I was also trying to figure out how to take care of you.

My best times at the hospital were during the day, when the nurses would bring you to my room. I would hold you in my arms for hours. You were circumcised the day after you were born. A nurse brought you in and said, "He needs mommy." The minute I held you in my arms you stopped crying. My God, what power I had. I was the mother tiger, lion, bear, and wolf. I thought I had all the basics to take care of you. All I had to do was to love you, spend time with you, and take care of you. I was not that scared anymore about what to do with you. Well, that was a very short-lived thought. I was totally wrong.

On the last night of a new mother's stay in the maternity ward, the hospital gave the new parents a special dinner. The last quiet supper! They set up a table with two chairs in my room with a white tablecloth, fine china, and the food we had chosen from the menu the day before. It was a farewell dinner from the hospital to the parents, and it was the last night we would eat alone for many years to come. The nurses took care of you while we enjoyed our dinner, well as much as I could since I was still in pain.

The next morning we packed everything, put you in your car seat, and drove back home. It was a bright sunny January day, with snow sparkling from the trees and rolling hills.

Thanks to the dean of the engineering school, I was teaching only one course that spring semester. I spent the rest of my time taking care of you. That gave us a chance to get to know each other. We had the fireplace burning every night to keep you warm. The rocking chair was right next to the fireplace. It felt so good to hold you in my arms while you were looking at me with those big eyes.

From January to May, during the whole spring semester, I was learning to take care of you, one step at a time. It was scary taking care of a baby with no guidance whatsoever. My sister was lucky. She had my mom to help with both of her children from birth until they grew up. I had nobody. Your dad was helpful during the day, but not at night, and he did not know what to do either. My nights were always broken into many little pieces of sleep. You never missed your 11 p.m. and 3 a.m. feedings, plus a few additional ones in between. For more than a year I tried every possible thing suggested by books to get you through a good night's sleep. But I had no luck. I was very tense.

During my classes, your dad would take care of you. You lucked out not having to go to daycare when you were really little. With all the pressure of being a new mom, being all alone, postpartum blues, and no close friends, I ended up drying up like a well. My milk got less and less each day. After the second month, you refused to take my milk and we put you on formula.

I was so excited when May came. I remember my first Mother's Day. I had you and would no longer be crying for not being able to have a baby. What a year! I became a mom. Your gift to me was yourself. I did not want anything else. Since your dad did not have time to drive to the nearest shopping center, which was an hour away, to buy a Mother's Day gift, he put a nice check in your hand and brought you over in your stroller. I was in the kitchen watching the spring bring new life to the trees. And here is my little life-form holding his first present for me.

The semester was almost ending, and I was getting ready for the finals and packing for our trip to Turkey. This time we were going together, just you and I. It had been a year since the Chernobyl accident. I packed our suitcases. And I, as a brave warrior, took you all by myself on your first trip to Turkey. You were only four months old. I remember the entire trip so vividly. I had to fly from Elmira, New York to Washington, D.C., then to Frankfurt, and then to Ankara. In some areas of the Frankfurt airport there were no escalators or elevators. I ended up carrying you, your diaper bag, your stroller, and your car seat, all together. I was cursing at the airport designers for not giving a damn about moms who handle everything like heavy-muscled porters. Boy, the things mothers can do for their children are unimaginable.

My dear family was excitedly waiting for your arrival. It was the arrival of little Bora to meet his extended family. You were the precious baby in my family, the one who came all the way from the far seas. We probably looked like we went through rough seas, avoided sirens, chopped Hydra's heads, and conquered countries. We were welcomed as the heroes of the year of 1988.

It must have been hard for my family not to meet you at your birth. They loved having you for three months. We had a great summer. After a few days in Ankara, we went to Taşucu, a Mediterranean village in the south of Turkey, to visit my grandfather, Kara Dede. After my grandmother died, he married a woman twenty years younger than he was. She was the widow of a police officer. She thought my grandfather would provide her with better financial security. My grandfather, as usual, exaggerated a bit regarding his fortune. He fibbed that he had acres of land and apartments. He did, but that was a long time ago. Actually, he was finally down to a point where he had nothing to sell. By that time, he already had sold his stone house to a developer to build an apartment building on the grounds of our big house and our big garden filled with fruit trees. They were all creations of my grandmother. While this ugly apartment construction was going on, the builder rented a house near the beach for my Kara Dede and his wife. The first night we arrived there, his wife started to spray every room with this mosquito-killing poison. The air became heavy with a chemical smell. I was really upset. I picked you up from your sleep and put you in your stroller. We took a long walk with my mom along the beach. The smell of the salty sea and the warmth of the evening were intoxicating. All I wanted then was to rent a place and never go back to the United States or to any other place. I wanted to raise you right there where everything smelled alive. I don't know why mothers think that a good education, a good job, and a city life are so important. And sometimes we sacrifice ourselves to get our kids educated, and then they sacrifice to get their kids educated. Sometimes, some of us should let go for once and see what happens. What would have happened if I did what I wanted to do that night? I would probably open a store or something there. And you would go to the one and only elementary school where there were only a handful of kids. But the rest of the time you could have fresh air, fresh food, friends, and maybe, fewer worries. No, there is something in us that prevents this. That is why my father became a mathematics teacher instead of being a fisherman or being a right hand for my grandfather. And that is exactly what I am doing now. And when you go back to your town, you see who stayed behind and did not break the chain. Some of them are happy and some of them are envious of you and your lifestyle, as if you had the best thing in the world. You also learn who left the town. Many of my cousins moved to other cities, and are all over the country. Except for me, I am in a different country. That is a whole different dimension.

One thing I want to make sure of is that you know your family and the country where your parents came from. You are the first generation born in the United States. Maybe, three or four generations from now, your heritage will not be passed from generation to generation, and things will be forgotten. For me, my family is unforgettable, with the good and the bad, living in a Mediterranean village and Ankara, with one leg, that is me, extended all the way to another continent and to another culture. And I would like to tell you our story from the beginning. Let me introduce you to a family from a little Mediterranean village called Taşucu.

2

Where My Genes Come From: My Family

Our family is a very close one. We three siblings, Aynur, Mehmet, and Nuray, spent a lot of time with each other, with our parents, and with our grandparents (especially on my dad's side), and with our uncles, aunts, and about thirty-eight cousins.

My Name

Of course you know my name. But, let me tell you where it came from. My dad named my sister Aynur. I assume there was no association with anyone in the family; it is just a beautiful name. When I was born, since my dad was a mathematician, he just created a permutation, and reversed the syllables and named me Nuray. The syllable *nur* means "divine light" and *ay* means "moon." So, my sister and I ended up with the same meaning in our names—"moon light." Although a number of belly dancers in Turkey choose their stage name as Nuray, I am still happy with my name.

My Parents' Wedding

My mom, of course, had an arranged marriage like everyone else in Turkey at that time. My father, after finishing college, heard about my mother—a beautiful red-haired, slim woman with a soft face, fair skin, and the softest personality you can imagine. My dad and his mother visited my mom's house to see the prospective bride. That was common. It was called *görücü*, which means the prospective groom and his family visit the prospective bride's house to take a look at her and to judge her by appearance and behavior in those few seconds of coffee-serving time. And this prospective bride is supposed to serve Turkish coffee to the guests. That was it: a glance that can only last a few seconds, and these few seconds will give you an idea if this person could be the one you would be spending the rest of your life with. This all happens during the coffee-serving time. The prospective bride does not sit down with the guests. She leaves the room and, if lucky, will try to eavesdrop to hear the voice of her prospective husband. It is a kind of lottery, or even a mysterious luck game. However, you should know that the prospective groom's family usually does a very thorough background check on the prospective bride's family. After the visit, the prospective bride's family does the same. As you know, one of the biggest tasks in a family is raising kids with good breeding and good behavior. So the measurement is solely based on how he or she looks and how good the family is.

My mother was so shy that she would not look up to see what my dad looked like. All she saw were my dad's socks. They were black.

Apparently my dad and his mother liked my mother and came back again with more relatives and asked my mother's father for her hand in marriage. My grandfather at least asked my mom if she was interested after they left. And my mom, surprisingly, said yes. She was famous for rejecting all other candidates before. My mom does not even know why she thought my dad was the one. Maybe the black socks?

After they became engaged, they could only see each other in the presence of another adult from the bride's side. They were married on October 14, 1953. Their relatives wished my parents to "age together on one pillow." In the old times in Turkey, couples used to share one long pillow in the bed. So when a couple got married, you would wish the couple to "age together on one pillow." During my childhood, the single pillow concept lost popularity, but the wish was still there. I wonder what people will think about the meaning of that wish when they forget that there used to be one pillow to share.

The summer of 1954 greeted my sister, followed by my brother in the spring of 1956, and then me in the summer of 1957. Three kids in three years. Three years and one day to be exact.

Three Babies in Three Years

My mother was not expecting my sister to be born until after the second half of July. So my father left her with my father's mother (who we called Büyükanne), and my father's grandmother, and went to teach summer courses to make some money. We used to call our father's grandmother

Ebe, which usually means "midwife." I still do not know why she was called Ebe. Her name was Havva (Turkish version of Eve).

Imagine there were just three women alone in Boklalan, our summer place at the top of the Taurus Mountains. My dad was in Tarsus teaching summer courses. My Kara Dede, my father's father, was in Taşucu doing the same thing he has done all his life, earning some money via trading (buying produce from the farmers and selling to large distributors), but unfortunately spending it faster than he earned it.

At Boklalan, with no doctor and no midwife, my mom went into labor, three weeks before her due date. She was a petite woman, very slim, about five feet three, and has a very thin bone structure and very small hips. She was always slender and soft, a perfect lady. Sometimes you feel like she is made out of the best porcelain in the world.

The labor was very hard. Only my Büyükanne and my Ebe could help her. They tied a rope to a tree. My mom was holding the rope to push. The labor lasted several hours. She lost a lot of blood. I bet she would have had a Caesarean section if she had been in a hospital. She and the baby were almost lost, including the future babies: my brother, me, and our kids. Think how one event changes so many things. It is the "butterfly effect," which ripples through an entire generation.

After all that tiring labor, just a day after my sister's birth, my Büyükanne asked my mom to get up and do house chores. I guess my grandmother thought my mom was one of those strong women who give birth while doing laundry by the river. Poor mom had no energy whatsoever. My Ebe, using her power as being the oldest mother-in-law, yelled at her daughter-in-law (my grandmother) to leave my mom alone. My Ebe was always protective of my mother against the blows of my Büyükanne and my dad.

My brother was born in April 1956 in Tarsus, less than two years after my sister. My sister was so jealous of the new arrival that she ran away to my parents' friends' house and stayed there a couple of days. She reluctantly came home, finally realizing that my brother was not just a visitor, but there to stay. A few months later, she was not happy about the attention that my brother was getting, especially that he was comfortably pooping into his diaper and no one was yelling at him. She decided to leave a perfectly coiled poop on my parent's white pillow.

Then your mother, that is me, came to this world in June 1957 in Tarsus. My sister had completely given up by then since there was no way that her statements would stop the influx of the new babies.

My grandmother stayed many months with us to help my mother in dealing with three babies—with no dishwasher, no washer, no dryer, no vacuum cleaner, no running hot water, and no disposable diapers. The workload was immense. Everything was labor-driven. I think that is one of the reasons parents helped their kids when they gave birth. This tradition is going away now, along with the joy of sharing the first few months of the incredible times with the babies. I promise you, if I am healthy and able, I will come and help you and your future wife.

My Mom

My mother constantly gave us nothing but love. She nurtured us, fed us, hugged us, and took care of us. She made soup and massaged our backs with hot olive oil when we were sick. She sat by us and held our hands when we were sad. She listened to us and she comforted us. My mom told us a lot of stories about herself, my dad, her parents, and our own mischief. It was a joy to listen to her stories.

Here is her life story, somewhat sad, but full of memorable events. It needs to be told, for we each carry a piece of my mom in our personalities.

As you know, she is the nicest person on earth. She never harmed anybody, never yelled at us, never said a bad word, and never criticized us. She only cursed once a year to my father on New Year's Eve when she had her "one glass of wine." She was always home, so we knew she would be there greeting us at the door when we came back from school. Always smiling, she never showed her sadness. She was content and happy with what she had, or maybe she just made us feel that she was content. She never said "I want . . . ." Maybe the way she lived her childhood made her content in every way possible.

My mom is one of two girls of eleven siblings. They were a big family. My grandfather had been married four times. My mother's oldest brother, Reşat Dayı (Uncle Reşat), had been in the army and retired as a colonel. He lived in İstanbul and married to a very nice lady from there. Their apartment, although a very modest one, was probably the most luxurious one among all the siblings. I loved visiting them, having breakfast on their balcony in Göztepe, İstanbul, the Anatolian side of the city, and being able to see the Bosporus while I ate my favorite breakfast items: bread, boiled eggs, feta cheese, jam, and olives. The next two of her siblings were twins: Abdullah Dayı and Ahmet Dayı. Abdullah Dayı had the same store that my grandfather had, and sold potatoes, onions, and baskets. He died falling off a ladder while fetching a basket hanging from a high shelf. Ahmet Dayı was an elementary school teacher, and he was my brother's first grade teacher. Then there were Hasan Dayı and Emin Dayı. Hasan Dayı was also a store owner. I am not sure, but he might have co-owned his father's store with Abdullah Dayı. Whenever we visited his store, if he had fresh fruit that day, he would offer it to us immediately. He would call us *yeğenim* (means "nephew or niece"). The word for nephew and niece is the same: *yeğen*. Emin Dayı had an office job at a hospital in Mersin, a coastal city very close to Silifke where my mother's family is from. These five uncles were from my grandfather's first wife. She died of a burst appendix. My grandfather then married his second wife, but it was a short marriage. She died during childbirth, and the baby also died. The last six siblings were from the third wife, Zehra Anneanne. These six siblings were very close in age, six babies in ten years, and very close in their friendship with each other. If I remember the order: Celal Dayı, Ihsan Dayı, my mother Lütfiye, Olcay Teyze (Aunt Olcay), Şahin Dayı, and Doğan Dayı. My grandfather died at the age of eighty-five, and was survived by his fourth wife and ten of his children. Abdullah Dayı died before him.

My mom's dad was a blonde, blue-eyed, tall, slim, and handsome man; we called him Sakallı Dede, meaning "grandfather with a beard." Later, he went to Mecca for his pilgrimage, and we started to call him Hacı Dede, meaning "grandfather who went to Hajj." He was very religious, and always had a beard, the type you see on the Muslim men. He was not a very close, loving father. He was a harsh disciplinarian, and had a posture that kept all his children and grandchildren away from him. We grandkids never felt close to him. He was just my mother's father. That was all. He had about thirty-eight grandkids, and I am sure he loved them all. Maybe he thought he could not divide his love into so many pieces and decided to spare a little for each one of us. Maybe, he did not even spare a speck. He was just the opposite of my father's father, with a larger-than-life personality, who had only four grandkids and loved to spend every minute of his life with them.

When Sakallı Dede was raising his kids, he had a tiny grocery store. He actually could have had a great future in the military. But he could not stand the smell of garlic. He left military school just because there was garlic in the food served at the cafeteria. He ended up opening a little shop to feed thirteen mouths. He was not at all a great merchant. The family suffered quite a bit, and lived in poverty. Somehow they all survived and made a living themselves. Since the age difference from oldest to youngest was big, about thirty years, the older ones supported the younger ones' education. Most of my uncles completed their college education. The two girls, my mother and her sister, were not allowed to continue their education after middle school.

My mother's mother died of ovarian cancer at the age of forty-two when my mother was just thirteen years old. It was caused by a piece left in her uterus when she had an abortion. My grandfather was so involved with his own life and love affairs that he ignored his wife's complaints about pain and heavy bleeding. I think he turned to religion after losing his wife to cancer.

I only know a little about my grandmother. Her name was Zehra. When she was fifteen or sixteen, she fell in love with a teacher. They got married right away. This happy young couple lived a nightmare year with his monster mother, who would not leave them alone. My grandmother could not bear the torture. She left her husband, who she loved very much, and went back to her family. Her husband died of tuberculosis a year later. He was probably torn between a monstrous mother and the lost love of his life. A couple of years later, when she was eighteen, my grandmother consented to marry a high-level judge, who was fifty-nine. They did not have any children. He was nice to her. After the judge died, she married my grandfather. She came to her new home with one of the most beautiful silver belts you could imagine. My mom always talks about how beautiful it was. Of course, it was sold to help support that little store and their already large family. Zehra Anneanne had six babies almost one after another. She did not have a great life taking care of eleven kids and a not-so-friendly husband.

My grandparents and the kids lived in a two-story house with wooden balconies on each floor. They mostly slept on the floor on thin cotton mattresses. Every morning they would fold their mattresses and bed covers and store them in a large built-in wardrobe. They had a kitchen with only one kerosene cooker. There were no cupboards, no refrigerator, and only a faucet on the wall at one corner of the kitchen where they washed the dishes. They ate on the floor surrounding a large brass round tray standing on a foot-high stand, called *sini*.

They also had a small two-room shack on the outskirts of Silifke, where they spent the summer months. I still do not know why they went there for summers; it was not even a summer retreat. The heat and humidity were the same as in Silifke, and they were not even closer to the Mediterranean. They called it Cökmedam, meaning "fallen roof." It fit its name. But somehow I loved that place. I remember sitting under a huge fig tree near the shack and eating freshly churned butter with hot flat bread (called *bazlama*) baked in an outdoor makeshift oven. And you would complement this amazing combination with a couple of freshly picked figs or watermelons. I will never forget the taste of that fresh butter. I am still in search of that butter, and have never found anything close to it. Sometimes, you would mix *bazlama* pieces with grape molasses (called *pekmez*) and butter to make the easiest and healthiest desert. I would lie down on a cot under the fig tree, looking up to locate a snake. I wanted to be like my mom so that I could tell stories of my bravery. When my mom was a teenager, she used to take walks with her girlfriends. On one of these walks, she spotted a large snake. The other girls screamed and started to run. My mom reached over, took hold of the tail, and shook it hard, so hard that all the bones were piled up, killing the snake. It is good to have a lot of brothers who can teach you how to be brave. That did not work very well for me, since my brother did not grow up with nature and was not really a hunter or a warrior. I still love him very much.

My mother was number eight in the children's age rank. When her mother died, she became the mother of the family at age thirteen—cooking, cleaning, and taking care of her father and her three younger siblings, who were devastated by the loss of their mother. Two of the siblings were very sick for a long time, so my dear mom swept all her grieving under a rug and just devoted herself to others for the rest of her life. She herself had quite a number of health complications in the years that followed. She did not live her childhood to the full extent. My grandfather did not send her to school after the eighth grade. At least she had a few close friends who helped her go through hard times.

Her father did not give her much freedom to stand up for her rights, to talk about her feelings, to be strong, to defend herself. She became a totally obedient person with a hidden stubbornness that she used to protect herself.

Sakallı Dede started a diary for each child he had from the day they were born. I happened to read my mom's last year. A very short diary, but very sweet. It is amazing to read something that was written starting in 1931 when my mother was born. My grandfather kept the diary until my mom and my dad got married. Then he gave it to them with a meaningful note telling them, "Now it is your turn to continue this diary." And my mom and dad started with their wedding day and included the first few years of their marriage, including the birth of their children. After that life got very busy and the writing stopped. Now I take that pen and continue with the stories that I heard from my mom and my own stories. This way I can at least bring you to the *avlu* of my family's house.

My mom was a great cook, and she was very keen about making us eat vegetables and fruits every day in addition to cheese, milk, meat, pasta and rice. She cooked for us and fed us all the time. We always had a wide variety of food. I still try to follow her way with meals today. We always have salad, a vegetable dish, a meat dish, pasta or rice, and always some soup in winter. All meals end with a fruit platter. The cost of food was the biggest expense in our family after my dad's gambling. There is even a great joke amongst us about my mom's food purchases. One day, she called a street vendor selling oranges on his cart door to door. Somehow, that day, we ended up with forty kilo of oranges. That is about ninety-six pounds of oranges. My father used to ask our visitors, "Why do you think my wife bought forty kilo of oranges that day?" Of course, no one could figure it out. The answer my father gave: "The vendor had only forty kilo of oranges on his cart." We had fresh orange juice for days.

We kept our healthy eating habits. Since we could not afford it, none of us was into clothing or entertainment, except maybe my father.

We also had our tradition of five o'clock tea time. From elementary school to the end of our college years, when we returned from our respective schools, after we were finished with homework, there was always this tea time when our family got together. Imagine nicely brewed tea in thin-bellied Turkish tea glasses. My mom would put together a tray of cookies, pies, or any other food that went well with the tea. There was always a tray of fruit. Sometimes, my mom would buy *simit*—a very thin bagel with sesame seeds, about a foot in diameter, and an inch thick, so the hole is much bigger than a bagel's—and serve it with feta or *kaşar* cheese.

Or she would make *börek,* consisting of layers of phyllo dough filled with either cheese and parsley, or ground beef with potatoes and parsley, or spinach and cheese. Our tea time was when we talked about everything. The circle at our talk time, our imaginary *avlu,* was mostly my mom, my brother, my sister, and I. Sometimes a few of our friends would join us. My dad would be either teaching somewhere or gambling at a club. We would not want him with us anyway. Our magic would be gone when he was present. We could not tell our father anything, since it would always be taken in the direction he wanted and we would be punished.

"Any little good deed you do will make you feel better." This was my mom's motto. Here is an example from one of the deeds that my mom told me about. There is this young cleaning lady, Fatma, who comes to my parents' house twice a week. Since my mom has Parkinson's disease, she needs a lot of help. Fatma cleans the house, cooks for my parents, bathes my mom, and goes grocery shopping for them. One cold rainy day Fatma came and, as usual, took her shoes off in the foyer, a Turkish custom, and started to work. When she was getting ready to leave in the evening, she realized that my mother had cleaned her muddy shoes while she was cleaning her own and my father's shoes. Fatma was surprised and asked my mom why she did it. My mom had the sweetest answer, "I did not want your shoes to feel bad about themselves amongst the clean and shiny shoes."

My mom was a delight. We could talk to her about anything. We would drink our tea, eat our goodies, and chat for an hour or more. Our dinners were around eight-thirty, so we would go back to our studies before dinner while my mom got the dinner ready. In the evenings, we watched television together. We three siblings grew up to be best friends. We still are. I think those tea times had a lot to do with it. We gave each other a shoulder whenever one wanted to cry; we shared our happiness and sorrow. I miss them dearly. I call my mom and my brother and sister almost every week. If I could afford it, I would call them every day. We visit Turkey twice a year and that is not enough at all for me. Seeing their faces at the airport is one of the greatest joys of my life. And leaving them behind always makes me cry. I am happy where I am, I am happy with most of my choices, but I still miss them. Now that I have come to some peace with my dad, still very limited, I even feel alright to spend a little time with him. Just a little though. Because, after a certain time with him, you really want to be alone for a couple of hours to unwind your twisted inner anxiety.

My Dad

This is a short summary about my dad. I left this section blank for a long time and came back to it again when I was almost finished writing. Maybe there is still a lot of anger in me that is holding me back from writing about him. He is a good grandfather now and he lost all his power, like an old wolf losing his teeth. I just want to include a few good memories of my dad so that you will get to know some of his good side.

My dad's salary was just a regular high school teacher's salary, even though he was teaching at the most prestigious high school in Turkey. To earn more money for his family he was also giving private math lessons to high school students on the side. He also might have been getting some bonuses that we did not know about, but all we knew was that for many years all we heard from my dad was that we could not buy anything.

I am sure that raising three kids with a teacher's salary must have been very hard for him. I remember for many years I used to have only two sweaters for the entire winter. To save money, mom continued to sew our clothes until we went to college. She even sewed winter coats for me and for my sister.

One morning in Ankara, when I was just seven, I saw my dad drinking beer. Given that he hardly drank, this was very unusual. My mom told me later that he took the bottle to the store to get the bottle refund to pay for his bus ticket to get his paycheck that day. I bet he could not pour the contents of the bottle into the sink, thinking that it would be a waste.

In Turkey anybody who works for the government, including all public school teachers, is called a *memur*. If you have a *memur* mentality, you stay within the confines of government, i.e., you have a guaranteed limited salary. *Memurs* are usually seen as no-risk takers, slow, bored, humble people who age quickly and retire early. Although my dad did not have any of these traits, he felt comfortable being a *memur* with the guaranteed salary. He had some opportunities to open tutoring centers, like Kaplan in the United States. However, he could not do it. He was offered equal partnerships from one of these centers, with no investment required from him besides his fame. He still could not do it.

It might be because of his father. He wanted to make sure that there was a steady income, even if it was a small one. My grandfather never worked for anyone. He had many jobs—from being a fisherman to owning an olive orchard to being a middle man, buying tomatoes from the fields and olives from the orchards and selling them to factories to make tomato paste and olive oil. However, in many cases he ended up spending or losing on gambling more than he earned, and my dad paid hefty amounts of my grandfather's debt. My grandfather literally relied on my dad to take care of his debts. And that never ended. That is also one of the reasons that we, the three siblings, never saw much money until we earned our own living.

I think I was about ten when my grandfather purchased a truck to deliver tomatoes to the factories. On its first trip, the truck flipped over and spilled all its contents. My grandfather has a picture of himself and the driver as if they were proud owners of a dead truck lying on its side. That is the way he was. He never worried about anything. My dad had to pay the bank the entire loan for the truck, the truck that did not even make a penny. This lasted many years, even causing my mom to patch our sheets many times over, literally patch over a patch. I never heard her complaining about this.

The only trait my father took from my grandfather was his gambling. They were both addicted to playing cards. This was a really bad addiction that hurt our family the most. He played almost every day for many years. He used to go to a private club, an apartment flat somewhere in the city, and play for hours. On the days my father won, he was happy. When he lost, we all stayed in our rooms and studied.

My brother and I realized that we had the same gambling trait when we were in grammar school. We loved playing cards. We vowed that we would never become gamblers and hurt our family. I still get so excited when I take a trip to Atlantic City twice a year. My eyes sparkle. But I can never do any damage to my family because of my unfortunate genes.

My Kara Dede

My Kara Dede, my father's father, was one of my best friends. He was an amazing positive force in our family, except for his debts, which made all of us suffer for many years. He loved spending money with or without us and loved taking trips. It was both fortunate and unfortunate for us, his descendants. We, especially the grandchildren, had a great time with him; we loved him. But we also watched his fortune disappear. He went from having a great deal of land and money to merely owning two mediocre apartment flats in a poorly built five-story apartment building on the lot where our 200-year-old stone house had once stood. Can you imagine, the builder painted the entire building purple, a bright ugly purple! You can see our apartment in Taşucu from every angle. It is like a symbol of our lost fortune.

We called him Kara Dede. Since we had two grandfathers, and in Turkish there is only one name, *dede,* we created different names for each. Sakallı Dede was very religious. He prayed five times a day. Kara Dede only prayed when there was a funeral or a religious holiday. Sakallı Dede hated Atatürk (the leader of Turkey). Kara Dede adored him. They hardly got along with each other.

I think Kara Dede was a symbol of modern Turkish man. He believed in all the reforms implemented under the leadership of Atatürk. These reforms were not at all small scale. They included changing of the Turkish alphabet from Arabic to Latin characters, allowing women the right to vote, abolishing special class privileges, bringing secularism, and many more.

Kara means "black" in old Turkish. Darker than plain black. Like the color of kohl. Well, my grandfather was not naturally dark skinned. He was just overly tanned from spending all his days outdoors in Taşucu, a beautiful idyllic village on the Mediterranean. The village is at the southernmost tip of the Turkish Mediterranean coastline. I guess the reason it is called Taşucu, meaning "stone tip," is that the entire landscape is covered with large rocks. There is even a stone quarry just outside the village, supplying materials for building stone houses and garden walls.

My Kara Dede had a cousin. They were both named Mehmet. To distinguish them, since one had a much lighter skin, they called Kara Dede's cousin Ak (means "white") Mehmet, and my grandfather, Kara Mehmet. When my grandfather established a pretty good position in the village, the villagers started to call him Kara Mehmet Aga. Aga is a common term given to highly respected people in villages. They usually own land and are sought after for advice. It is kind of a combination of a rich man and a wise man. The Aga remained with him even after he got so dirt poor that my father had to support him fully. But he was always Aga, the wisest person in Taşucu.

Kara Dede was a very charming person and was friends with everybody, including the only "lady of easy virtue" in the town! And he considered his grandkids, four of us—three siblings plus my cousin—his greatest achievements. He loved us unconditionally, and he would do anything to spend time with us. He was the most influential character in my life. He was born in 1905 and died in 1999 at the age of ninety-four. He was a walking historian. I loved listening to his stories of World War I (when Anatolia was divided and taken over by British, Italian, French, and Greek forces), the Turkish Independence War, Mustafa Kemal Atatürk, first automobiles, fishing, trading, olive orchards, science, nature, cooking, drinking, smoking, walking, hugging, smiling, doing it your way no matter what they say, standing up for your rights, anything you can think of. I learned a great deal from him.

My grandmother used to call him *aferin delisi*, meaning "crazy for just praise." She was always mad at him because he would give huge loans to people and would never try to get the money back. And many of these loans were never returned. He would donate land to poor people to build houses on. I even watched him give his pickup truck to his driver in exchange for getting a free ride whenever he wanted. This is how the driver paid back the cost of the truck to my grandfather: just driving him around. After a few years, the driver decided that he had paid his loan and he stopped giving rides to us.

He always wore the same style clothes, totally fashion-free, very practical—a short-sleeved, thick, broadcloth light brown shirt with two big chest pockets that would hold his glasses and his money. The pants were the same color and the same fabric. He wore black or brown shoes and thin socks. He always had short hair, which got thinner and thinner as he got older. He had a strong presence. He had long lean legs and a thick torso, not fat, but wide shoulders and chest. He had big soft hands. He had a permanent tan line on his arms from the short sleeves. He hated taking baths. Anybody living with him always had to force him to take a bath, especially during summer months. He averaged about one bath every two months. When he came out of the bathroom his tan would be three shades lighter. And my mom used to scrub the bathtub after his bath to get rid of the grime.

He sweated constantly. He loved spicy food; actually he loved any kind of food. He used to start sweating with the sight of chili peppers. He would fold a newspaper in a doughnut shape and put it under his peasant cap so that the newspaper would absorb the grease off his head. It was his morning ritual after first reading the newspaper.

He was the most liberal person I have ever met. When my brother told him that his dear granddaughter, that is me, was getting married to an American, his comment was, "Nuray knows how to knock down artificial country borders. She is truly global. I know she will be very happy."

I got married the year he died. I knew that he did not have much time left. I took my husband Al to see him as part of our honeymoon. My dear Kara Dede was ready to greet him and hug him. I held his hands during our short visit with him. I was happy that he had met my husband and that we got his blessing. It was my last time seeing him and he was still full of joy and life. I am happy that I got to have him as my grandfather. Memories of him will always be vivid with me. One of the reasons I am writing this is so that you will know me better, and know the most influential person in my life. You met him only a few times. I wish I had taken you to see him more often.

He had his jokes ready. He asked me to translate to Al. I was afraid of what was coming, since my grandfather was never embarrassed and never set limits on his jokes! Here is one of the jokes he told Al: "Why do you think camels need human beings as much as humans need camels?" Silence from us with a smile on our lips. "Men need camels to do the hard work. Camels need men for their pleasure, to hold their penises in a proper way to have sex." I looked up on the internet to find out if this is true. I could not find anything. But, I remember that Aidan Hartley, in *Zanzibar Chest*, mentions a good deal about camels and their penises being backwards. Just to clarify one thing, Turkey does not have many camels. There are only a few for tourist attractions to give rides and for the camel fights. So the ad showing a picture of a camel on the Camel cigarette pack and saying "blend of Turkish tobacco" is absolutely misleading.

Another joke was to ask Al, "Who is the only person in Taşucu who is older than me?" Of course, I knew the answer. "The only 'lady of easy virtue' in Taşucu." And he spent a good deal of time with her. She ended up outliving him. Kara Dede told us a few stories of his time with her as if those were casual stories that could be told to grandkids. He said he would snatch a chicken from our chicken coop and take it to her house with the chicken's legs dangling, live, with feathers and all. My grandmother would think that one of our chickens ran away again. The "lady of easy virtue" would cook the chicken and serve it with some *meze* and *rakı*, a traditional Turkish drink, and they would have a night with music and food and . . . !

My grandfather got married at the age of sixteen to my grandmother who was nineteen. My grandparents had two children, my father and his elder sister who died when she was nineteen.

My Kara Dede's mother Ebe lived with them for many years. She died at the age of eighty-eight. I remember her very well. But I don't remember the year she died. I must have been around nine or ten then. She was as nice as my grandfather. I would sit by her and just talk to her. She was soft-spoken, always quiet with a caring face. She had two of the same style dresses that my mother used to sew for her. They were long dresses, flannel for winter and cotton for summer, with pockets and a few front buttons at the bosom for easy removal. No ironing needed. My mom used to sew my grandmother's dresses too. Our Ebe used to spin wool into thread all day long; she talked little but understood a lot. She was a wise old woman, and we loved her dearly. Since her eyesight was very poor, I guess spinning wool was a good thing to do to make one's self a contributor to the family. I don't remember what she did with all that spun wool. I bet my grandmother made ropes or sweaters out of it.

Kara Dede never went to school. He learned how to read and write while serving in the military, which is a mandatory service for all young men reaching eighteen. However, he never stopped learning. He always read the newspaper, and he always listened to the news and commentaries. He loved politics. He was a key figure in the town council.

An Unforgettable Story: My Trip with My Kara Dede

The day of my first trip outside the country started with my arrival at Taşucu around five in the morning. I found my Kara Dede, as usual, playing cards with his friends in a coffee shop. The minute he saw me, he folded his hand and left the table without saying a word to his fellow players. He asked me if I was interested in taking a trip that day to Cyprus and said that the ferry was leaving at noon. I was so excited. But I did not have a passport. He did not have one either. He called a taxi and he gave the driver a roll of money and two of my passport-size photographs, which I always had in my wallet. Since every official document required a picture, many people carried these passport-size photographs with them all the time. The taxi left at around seven in the morning to go to Mersin, about an hour away, and came back at eleven with two passports. We were on the ferry at noon.

Kara Dede was friends with everyone from age "seven to seventy-seven." That is how he described himself. As a natural extension, he was friends with the owner of the ferry service between Taşucu and Girne in Northern Cyprus. That helped us get a free ride on the ferry on the captain's deck. It was a small ferry carrying about ten cars. It had a small enclosed seating area on the lower deck and a large seating area on the upper deck. We boarded the ferry with two small bags, enough to hold two days' clothes. There were a couple of people who were traveling with us, and they had their car so that we could easily travel in Cyprus.

Our "smooth" six-hour ride turned into a wild ride in no time. The ferry was bobbing in and out of the waves like a walnut shell. Everything on the decks was washed out including the big searchlight in front of the ferry. Cars were all chained so they were just bumping around a bit. Most of the passengers got seasick, including the captain. Kara Dede and I could not go into the enclosed area where all the passengers were. The stench of the vomit was so strong that we knew we would be sick too. So we stayed on the upper deck and held tightly onto a post and let the waves come down on us over and over again. I don't remember how long it lasted. I remember many times the captain asking us to steer for him so he could check his engines or throw up overboard. It was almost like a game for me at the age of seventeen. I am not sure I could face a storm the same way today.

The sea started to calm down by the time we saw the Girne harbor. There were many boats circling us, and a rescue helicopter was hovering above us asking if anyone got hurt. I realized my legs were shaking and all my clothes, including my underwear, were wet when we got out of the boat. Wet and tired, we found a hotel on the harbor, changed our clothes and went for a fabulous dinner. Actually we had two dinners that night to celebrate our survival. What is a better way to celebrate being alive than eating good food with good company? Kara Dede was just like me, or was I just like him? A hedonist, or just an epicurean. We love food and we love company and we enjoy life. In the first restaurant we had Adana kebab, grilled very spicy ground meat with tomatoes and peppers. We washed the heat down with cold beer. Then, we had a feast on a bottle of Yakut, a wonderful red Turkish wine, two perfectly grilled fresh fish, delicious salad, and warm bread. We talked about almost everything. He truly was one of my best friends. What I could not dare to share with my father, from just going out to movies with my friends, my feelings, my fears, my happiness, my growing up, from life to science to people, I shared with my grandfather. I never had a conversation with my father on any topic except a daily "how are you?" and yelling, but with my grandfather all was different.

A Lesson from My Kara Dede: My First Drink

When I was thirteen and visiting my grandparents, as I always did in summer, my Kara Dede told me that he would take me out to lunch. It was a very hot summer day, noontime, not a leaf moving, with the temperature above 100 degrees. He took me to the restaurant on the beach run by one of his friends. It was not even a restaurant. A couple of wooden tables on the sand with a few wooden wobbly chairs under a shade made out of date branches. He ordered some food and two large bottles of Efes Pilsen, one of the two brands of beer you could find in Turkey. It is actually an excellent beer. It was ice cold and delicious. So I drank it like water with my meal. Boy, it hit me hard. Real hard. I could not talk or walk straight. I tried to wake myself up in the sea, which was hopeless given that the sea temperature was around eighty-five degrees—just lukewarm. I almost drowned. I ended up throwing up on the sand and getting a really bad headache. He told me after all this misery that this was a lesson for me. There is an old Turkish saying: "It doesn't stay the same as it stays in the bottle." My dear Kara Dede showed me what it means to get drunk and lose control of yourself. He said: "Unfortunately, this world is not meant to be equal for boys and girls. There will always be differences no matter how much we try."

He wanted me to be ready for any unfair situations I might face in the future and to be able to protect myself from anything bad that might happen. This was a good lesson, almost like a scientific experiment in a controlled environment. And since that day, although I love wine—not beer though—I have always been careful not to go overboard.

This was not the only incident my Kara Dede helped me with. He helped during my adolescence. He was the one who bought me my first bikini, even though my dad tried with all his might to stop him. He was the one who bought me my first calculator during the times when they were very expensive. He was the one who always told me that he trusted me no matter what. And I did not let him down. He was never upset if I showed up late at night, since he always knew where I was. I loved him dearly, and I still miss him.

Excitement: Kara Dede's Motorcycle

Kara Dede bought his last motorcycle at the age of seventy-two, and sold it at the age of seventy-five after my cousin had an accident on it. He was afraid that his grandkids would get hurt! He used to take me to the movies at night. With the summer night breeze on our backs, we would arrive at the movie theater with our motorcycle, under everyone's stare. We would buy sunflower seeds and sit on the wooden chairs and watch the old double-feature low-budget "Bollywood" style Turkish movies at the open-air movie theater. At the end of the movie, our chairs would be on a pile of sunflower seeds shells. He was a great sport in everything we did together.

Technology: Kara Dede's Phone Number

Somehow the story of how telephones got introduced to Taşucu stayed fresh in my memory. Back in the late1960s they brought a telephone line to Taşucu. In the first few months, the only way you could make a call was to go to the post office, staffed by one person. You asked her to place a call for you. She would crank the handle of this black phone that you usually see in old movies. She would talk to the operator on the other end, the city that you were calling, and the two operators would connect the two parties. Later, they started to bring telephone lines to homes. My Kara Dede, always a pioneer, got the second phone in town, with the first phone being at the mayor's office. Our phone number was 2. And it was the same black phone that the post office had. We would crank the handle, connect to our operator, and give the number for her to dial. The phones in Ankara were of course, more advanced. You could make a house-to-house call. However, from Ankara we could not dial my Kara Dede directly; we needed to go through the Taşucu post office. The lady would know where he was, would even tell us if my grandfather was having lunch at a restaurant across the street, or he left town for a few hours. She sometimes would shout to call him to the telephone or would connect to my grandfather's house. It was a small town and he was such a small-town celebrity.

We also had a very old radio. My brother still has it. When I was little, I thought there were tiny people living in the radio who would make all the sounds. And I would dream about how they would live in that big wooden box. And what would they do when the radio was turned off? Would they go to sleep? What would they eat? I imagined that they played tiny musical instruments.

While my grandfather was keeping up with technology, my grandmother was thinking that all of these weird devices were the products of the devil.

My memories with him are always with me. The smell of certain foods, flowers, the gentle laps of waves on the shore, and long hot peppers are great reminders of my carefree great times with him. I will carry them with me every day wherever I go.

At my last visit, all I wanted was to see his face, hold his hands, stroke his soft cheeks, and say my farewells to him. I wanted him to see me happy. My last glimpse of him was his waving from the balcony of the second-floor apartment where once stood our grand stone house. He died a few months later.

I still cherish one of his presents and cannot be without it during winter. It is that soft plush blanket he gave me as an engagement gift when I was twenty-two. Since then I have used that blanket every day during cold winter nights either on my bed or cuddled up in it while watching television or reading a book. That blanket survived a trip from Turkey in 1981 and six surgeries and many illnesses. It hugged me and gave me comfort when I needed it the most. I thank him for everything, including keeping me warm.

Büyükanne

We called our grandmother *Büyükanne*, which means "big/grand mother", instead of *Babaanne*, which means "father's mother." She was our father's mother, of course. However, we had a cousin who lived with us after his mother, my father's sister, died when he was two. And I guess we found a common grandmother name to eliminate confusion, rather than three of us saying Babaanne, and the other one saying Anneanne. But, since my cousin's father got remarried and totally ignored him, my cousin spent many years with us and with my grandparents. He ended up calling his grandmother *Anne* and his grandfather *Baba*.

My Büyükanne's name was Meryem (Turkish version of Mary). She lived a very simple life. I don't think my grandmother ever owned a dining room table and chairs inside the house. We had an old table and broken chairs outside when we ate outside. In the house, we ate on the floor with a clean tablecloth spread on the kilim rug and a *sini* (serving tray) on the tablecloth. You place a foot-high support under the *sini* to raise it a bit off the floor so that when you sit your knees do not go over the tray. You place part of the tablecloth over your knees to use as one giant napkin to share. That was fun for me, different from what I had at our Ankara home, where we sat around a regular table with our feet dangling. Spending weeks in my grandparents' house was like playing in a doll house.

I always thought my grandmother was from the ancient times. She never went to school and never learned to read and write. Even the words she spoke were ancient Turkish words that many people would not understand. Both of my grandparents were very smart people, especially my grandmother. I bet she could have been a successful surgeon if she ever had the chance to go to school. I saw her do two operations on our animals. She removed a fish bone stuck deep in our cat's throat, and she operated on a chicken that would not lay eggs and screamed all day with pain. She relieved the chicken somehow and fixed the egg-laying problem.

When she was younger, she made all of her fabrics from raw silk or fine spun soft silk. From these fabrics, my mother made an entire silk sheet set for my sister when she was getting married. I still have her silk fabrics and cannot even use them. They stay in my linen closet, and I think about her every time I see these fabrics. I will give them to you when you have your own house.

She made her own soap from olive oil and caustic (lye). That was a nasty process. White steam came out of the caustic when it was mixed with water. She poured the mix of olive oil and caustic into a tray to dry under the lemon tree. The soap was pure with no additives. I even washed my hair with it. It was gentler than the best shampoo. Isn't it amazing that you use olive oil soap to wash your oily hands?

One summer, when I was about fifteen, my sister and I were in Taşucu. Somehow, we were out of soap. We started to search the entire house trying to figure out where our Büyükanne would hide the bars of soap. We found a nicely folded, soft white cloth with a nice big bar of soap, probably the best one she ever made. We enjoyed the suds of this amazing soap for a few days. Büyükanne finally realized what we were using. We ended up drying the remainder of that soap bar and putting it back. We were using the soap she reserved for her own corpse to be washed with! That soft white cloth was her *kefen,* which would be used for wrapping her corpse before the burial.

She also made her own extra virgin olive oil. We had large glass bins to store our own olive oil. My parents would take several containers to Ankara, and that would be our olive oil for the whole year. Extra virgin olive oil has this beautiful greenish yellow color and a strong taste. Now, finally, the United States appreciates the beauty of olive oil and prices have come down reasonably. I am enjoying the same feeling I had when I was a little girl. I remember my grandmother whenever I pick up a bottle of olive oil.

Büyükanne had a full setup in front of our house to extract olive oil. I would go to our orchard with my grandmother, my mother, my brother, and sister along with our donkey. My grandmother would spread sheets under the trees, and with long sticks we would hit the branches and the olives would fall down, all shiny and green, like gems. We would eat our lunch under the trees. Somehow, our olives would be brought in from our orchard. I am not sure how, but perhaps via a borrowed tractor. We would spread the olives on the circular stone. After crushing the olives under the giant stone wheel with the aid of our donkey, my grandmother would transfer them to the seven layers of stone pools. Olive oil would drip from one pool to another, getting more purified at each layer. It would come out as this dark greenish yellow oil that was ready to use.

She also made her own bread for many years until she was too old to handle it. She used to yell at us if we ever bought bread from the bakery. She thought it was outrageously expensive. Since she was used to growing her own vegetables, raising her own livestock, having her own olive orchard and tiny vineyard, and spinning her own wool and silk, she did not need to buy anything from the market. The only food items she would buy were flour, salt, and, since she did not have cows, milk and yogurt from a villager. This is the same villager who my grandfather gave land to as a gift. The family still lives in the house they built themselves on that land. He would come every morning and bring fresh milk and yogurt for our daily consumption. Anything that required money was expensive for my grandmother. She also would sell her excess vegetables, mostly tomatoes, to the neighbors. She would tie her earnings in a handkerchief and stuff it in a hidden pocket of her dress. My Kara Dede always found a way to convince her to give him her money, which he spent on gambling.

Besides making *bazlama* (flat bread), my grandmother had monthly baking days. She and my mother would sit for hours across a fire, even in the hot summer days, to make *yufka*, a very thin, delicate flat bread, as thin as a tree leaf. It was baked on a round, flat, dome-like metal tray, called *saç*, placed on a wood fire. These leaves of *yufka* were then stacked neatly in a corner in a pile reaching almost six-feet high. There were hundreds of them in the pile. We would cover them with clean cotton tablecloths to keep the dirt out. When it was meal time, we would take a few, put them in the middle of a tablecloth, sprinkle them with water to soften them, and cover them with the folds of the tablecloth. We would wait for a while until they were softened, fold them in squares, and make a pile ready to eat.

During all those years my grandmother hated housework. She would complain and yell at everyone when she did any work inside the house. The only place she was really happy was outdoors. She would spend hours in the garden. I have vivid memories of her bending over, picking tomatoes while cursing at my grandfather for taking her money. There was a date tree right at the entrance to our house adjacent to the concrete landing. My grandmother hated that tree because of all the fallen dates on the clearing. She would wash the front of the house and the concrete landing with a hose and a broom a few times a day. She would constantly mutter about it. To end her agony, she ended up having it cut, ignoring our protests. My brother saved a piece of the trunk to make a flower pot.

She would make her own grape molasses and tomato paste for winter. The grapes from our tiny vineyard in Boklalan would be crushed, strained, and boiled in a big pot over a fire built in our front yard. It would take hours and hours to turn the thin grape juice into a thick, rich grape molasses, with no pesticides or additives.

We had a big tomato patch. I remember watering those tomato plants every day. At the end of my task, I would pick one or two to eat, just like apples. The taste of those tomatoes picked warm from the sun was amazing. When September harvest time came, she would have all of us work round the clock to pick all the remaining tomatoes. Then they would have the same destiny as the grapes, being slowly simmered outdoors under the sun. Again, the thick tomato juice would turn into delicious tomato paste, which my mom would turn into delicious dishes. So, when we returned to Ankara, just before the schools opened, we would have our yearly supply of olive oil, crushed green olives, oil-cured black olives, tomato paste, grape molasses, soap, big bushels of lemon, pomegranates, dates, walnuts, peanuts, cheese, sesame seeds, dried herbs, mountain tea (from a sideritis plant)—you name it. I loved that mountain tea. When you steep it in hot water, the water turns into an aromatic bright yellow tea, very soothing for your stomach and a great cure for your cold. It is almost impossible to find it in the United States.

My Sister Aynur

Being the oldest in the family, my sister Aynur will always be my second mother. I call her *Abla*, meaning "older sister." I never call her by her first name. She is your Aynur Teyze, your Aunt Aynur. The only one.

My sister married very young, when she was about twenty-one and still in medical school, to a great brother-in-law, Güngör. He was our Güngör Abi, our big brother. We all loved him dearly as a real brother until he died of lung cancer. He was only forty-two.

My sister and Güngör Abi met at the Ankara bus terminal. My sister was on a break from medical school and was traveling to Taşucu to visit my grandparents. My dad took her to the bus terminal and saw Güngör Abi taking the same bus. My dad knew Güngör Abi's family. He asked Güngör Abi if he would take care of my sister until she got on the local bus to Taşucu. My dad was always worried when his girls traveled alone. My sister and Güngör Abi talked all night on the bus ride. A few months later, his family asked my parents for her hand in marriage. Then, this great couple dated for several months, fell in love and got married. Juggling newlywed life and the heavy burden of medical school, she was able to complete her medical degree.

My brother and I used to visit them in their first apartment. We were always welcomed with a great smile from them. We would eat dinners and watch television shows. Their house became my second retreat after Taşucu.

Two days after my sister finished medical school, I went with her to her doctor to get a blood test done and got the great news. She was pregnant with her first baby. We hugged and hugged for a long time. She was so happy. I was too. This was going to be the first baby in the family.

My sister spent a few months in İstanbul, staying with one of my uncles to complete her mandatory internship. Nine months passed quickly for us, but I am sure it was not the same for my sister. She used to send me to get candied chestnuts. She had enormous cravings for those. Her nine months turned into ten months and the doctor decided to induce her labor. The day my sister was scheduled to have her labor induced, she went into labor by herself. We took her to Ankara University Medical Faculty Hospital where one of her friends, a gynecologist, was on duty. While everything was progressing at a normal pace within the painful standards of having a first baby, the power went off at the hospital. And the generator was in repair. This was very common in Ankara then. The generators were in constant maintenance and repair. My dad rushed home to get flashlights and a lantern, and my sister had my nephew under the flashlights. Lights came on halfway through delivery. Tolga came out all wrinkled with long fingernails grown during his extra thirty days in his mom's tummy. The entire medical faculty was at my sister's bedside the next morning. He was incredibly cute.

I loved him from day one. My sister and Güngör Abi wanted to be close to my parents so that my mom would take care of Tolga during the day. So they moved to the same apartment building where my parents lived. My brother and I were still attending college and living with our parents. My parents were on the fourth floor and my sister was on the third. My mother took care of Tolga for many months, but it was too much for my mother to manage two houses. She cooked for eight people, since we all ate together. Tolga was quite a rascal and kept her running after him all day. We tried to send him to a daycare center, but that did not work out somehow. We ended up hiring a nanny, a young girl named Elif. That worked well. My mom could check on them anytime and have Elif and Tolga for breakfast, lunch, and at tea time. Then we would all have dinner together.

I remember one of the horrifying events regarding Tolga. I was home early from school and Elif came to me all worried and said something was wrong with Tolga. Tolga was in terrible pain, crying and telling us that his stomach hurt. He was all curled up and we could not touch his stomach to rub him or comfort him. I felt this needed something beyond a house remedy. I called my sister at her hospital and then called my brother at his hospital. My brother immediately brought the top gastroenterologist to my sister's home. The doctor thought Tolga's intestines were somehow blocked. He said it was a dangerous case, and he would need surgery immediately. The doctor wanted to examine Tolga further to identify the location of the blockage. He put a plastic glove on and checked Tolga. Somehow, like a miracle, Tolga's face changed and he turned to me and said "silly Teyze." He used to call me that when he was in a good mood. My sister still thanks me for saving Tolga's life and having him recover without surgery. I think we just lucked out that the examination became the cure.

A few years later my sister and her family moved to Bolu. Bolu is one of the old cities in Turkey that was built in a valley surrounded by mountains, with beautiful lakes and forests. Lots of snow and lots of water. Every time I visited my sister, we used to discover yet another great spot to spend the day. My sister became a very well respected doctor there. Six years later a second baby, my one and only niece, Derya, arrived. I was already in the United States when my sister had her. I saw Derya when she was six months old. Very cute, with lots of hair. She still has the most beautiful hair in the world. It is so thick that when she washes her hair it does not dry for two days.

Everything was going smoothly with my sister as in any good functioning family. I was really happy for her. They were an adorable family. They ended up having lots of friends in Bolu. Money was no object. She was making a very good income, with patients coming from all around Turkey.

Unfortunately, one dreadful day in the summer of 1990 my sister received a call from Güngör Abi's workplace. They had taken him to the hospital. He had trouble walking and concentrating. Diagnosis: brain metastasis. Later tests revealed that he had cancer that had spread from his lungs to his brain, and it was too late for any cure. The doctors gave him nine months to live. We even took his test results to the cancer centers in New York in case there was a chance for a cure if we brought him here. Nothing. He melted away in those nine months. I wanted to see him alive one more time. I arrived on a cold early March day. I could not believe my eyes. How much weight can a person lose? That handsome, strong person turned into an old man with pajamas covering only his bones and skin. While I was there he was hospitalized, which meant death was near. He was in so much pain and needed hospital care. My sister and the two kids came to my parents' house to stay. We did not want to send my sister to her home alone with two children. We told the kids that night.

I remember my sister, my mother, and I were in the room that I used to share with my sister. We had two mattresses on the floor for the kids. The room where my sister and I shared our secrets and loves became a room we shared the worst news with her kids. It was so hard to tell them. They cried and asked a lot of questions. They still wanted some hope that their dad might live.

The next day I picked up the kids from their schools and took them to a local cafe. We ate lunch and talked for a long time. I wanted to make sure they were alright before I took them to their dad, maybe for the last time. Tolga wanted to cheer up his dad and bought a joke book from a little dusty bookstore near his school. It is heartbreaking to see how kids try their best to make others happy when things really go bad. At the hospital, he tried to read pages from the joke book while we were watching Güngör Abi suffer from pain. The medications were not enough.

I stayed with my sister for a week. I had to come back. Two days after I left, the doctors recommended sedating Güngör Abi. My sister told me later that she asked him before he was sedated if he had anything to say to her. "Forgive me all my mistakes. I love you." That was all he said. My brother and my sister took turns to stay with him at night. My brother was with him the night he died. I received a call from my sister the next morning. I wished I was there with her. Many years passed until my sister could date again. However, Güngör Abi will always have his special place in our hearts.

My Brother Mehmet

Being so close in age, only fourteen months apart, my brother and I grew up like twins. He was only a year ahead of me at school. Many years we walked to school together. I knew all of my brother's friends very well. When he went to boarding school for high school, I felt alone. At least he used to come home on the weekends.

My mom always told us that he was the quietest among the siblings. He was never a daredevil. He had a big head when he was little, which looks perfectly normal now. Since his head was big, he would have trouble playing. He had many bumps on his head, especially when he played with his plastic yellow bus with a string attached. He would pull the yellow bus going backward, and any stone he encountered going backward made him get another bloody head. He also had a strange bone structure. Any time he wrestled with one of our cousins, he would get a dislocated joint. We once counted seven dislocations in five months. At that time, you would not go to a doctor for dislocations. There were "dislocation fixers" in town, and they would come and put your joints back together.

He was the only one in the family whose talents and interests were cultivated. He was in the table tennis team of his high school. He taught me how to play table tennis on my parent's dining room table. He taught me the spins, slams, tricky serves. I still cherish those lessons when I play with my husband. My dad bought him a guitar when he was ten. I don't remember whether my brother asked for it, or my parents thought it would be good for him. No matter what, my sister and I were always left behind in any of these activities. We were not allowed to have music lessons. We were not allowed to join a sports team, even though we were both asked to be on the school's basketball team. We were not allowed to have a bicycle of our own. Mehmet had the only bicycle. He was never a heavy biker, so my sister, the real daredevil in the family, would take my brother's bike for spins around the neighborhood.

His music interest developed during his high school years and flourished during college. He and I would make music together for hours. He would play his favorite instrument, the ud, and I would sing all the Turkish songs. I still remember most of the lyrics. Since I moved to New Jersey, we attend the Turkish New Year ball every year. All my memories with my brother come back to me when the musician starts playing the Turkish songs. My friends and I gather around a table and start belting out all the songs that represent the time, in the 1980s, when we all left to come to the United States. We all go back in time and turn into young high school or college kids living back in Turkey.

He met his wife Özden at a seaside motel at the Marmara Sea. Özden was the daughter of the motel owner. Mehmet probably fell in love at first sight, but did not stay long enough to introduce himself. The following year, he asked his friends to go back there to see this girl again. He was almost finished with his medical education and he was probably thinking it was about time to be serious about dating. Somehow the word about Mehmet's interest in her reached Özden. Since she had never met him before, she thought he was a short, ugly, little guy with spectacles, a typical "nerd doctor" look. She had her share of surprise when she first met him. They got engaged the year I came to the United States. I missed the whole party. They got married a year later. I missed that too.

They are now happily married with a late arrival of a little son, Firat. After living carefree, their lives have changed drastically. They hope that Firat will be just like you. You have a special place in your uncle's heart.

My dear Al describes Mehmet as a funny guy who likes to drink *rakı* and tell jokes. Of course, the jokes are in Turkish. Al watches Mehmet's face change as the story develops and then enjoys the belly laughter that my brother releases. My job is to translate all of it to Al without missing the essence of the joke. This is a hard job, you know. We never get bored when we have dinner with him, even though one side of the table gets quiet while I translate what they say to the other side. Then we all laugh together.

My favorite moments with him are having long dinners, by the seashore, where the restaurant owner places our table and chairs right next to the water, sometimes in the water. He loves *rakı* and he loves company. We never run out of topics.

One Family Reunion

I held my promise to my mom and went to see her in November 2005 for a week. My brother drove from Datça with his family. We all stayed at my parents' house. My sister came every day. One of the biggest highlights of my visit was that we three siblings went to the movie theater together. The three of us sat next to each other and watched a Turkish movie reflecting the time when we were in college. The music, the historical events were right in front of our eyes shown on the big screen. Once in a while we looked at each other with disbelief. Just as in the old times, my brother again asked my sister zillions of questions about the movie. We giggled every time he asked a question. Probably the last time we had done this was thirty years ago. It was a strange feeling, as if nothing changed.

After the movie we came home. My mom, as usual, had the tea ready. My dad got up from his afternoon nap. At that moment there were only five of us in the house. Only the seed family. Time was frozen and brought back all of our memories. We all felt it. We could not believe that we could recreate the same atmosphere after thirty years. We immediately fell into our old roles. We even ended up sitting logistically the same way we did thirty years ago. My brother, my sister, my mother, and I were at the dining table chatting and drinking tea. My father was sitting by the window, trying to cut into the conversation with his perpetual criticism on every topic we talked about and eating pomegranates with loud lip smacks.

We all hate the eating sounds that people make. I know why now. After all those years of getting irritated with my dad's eating sounds, we developed a strong correlation between the sounds a person makes while eating and the arguments and fights that start right after that. So it happened again. My brother asked him to eat with less noise. My dad got upset, as he always did for many years. In the past we thought that was his way of justifying his trip to the gambling club almost every night. Maybe he did this on purpose so that he could act frustrated and leave the house. And that night he did the same thing. He put his coat on, cursed under his breath, and left home. And just like thirty years ago, we all felt the same sense of relief.

3

Places of My Childhood

On your first trip to Turkey, I was proud to show you off. This little beautiful thing was coming from a faraway place visiting his ancestors' grounds. We landed in Ankara. I took you to Taşucu and Çınarcık. Every place I went, I wanted to pour my memories into your little mind so that you could remember them in the future. You were so little then. As the years passed, you learned to appreciate the beauty and the warmth of the people and the land.

Introducing the Mediterranean

On your first trip to Turkey in 1988, we took off with two cars from Ankara to Taşucu to see my grandparents and my wonderful village. It was your first long car trip. There were no air conditioners in the cars. You had on a little onesie and a wet napkin on your head to keep you cool. We stopped a lot to cool you under the shade of eucalyptus trees. When we came to the Taurus Mountains, the landscape changed. After miles and miles of yellow grain fields, rippling waves through the grain under the hot breeze, we reached the pine forests. The weather got cooler, and the smell changed. You could faintly smell the sea from the other side of the mountains. I remember when I used to take the bus from Ankara to Taşucu, I loved the feeling when we reached the Taurus Mountains. In winter, everything would start turning whiter and whiter, eventually with snow accumulations of a few feet, softly rolling over hills, and weighing down the beautiful pine trees. In summer, the white soil would sparkle under the moonlight, reminding me of the cold winter travels to Taşucu.

This time we took a daytime trip. I could see all the places that I had not seen in years. There were oleander bushes alongside the road with pink and white blossoms. There were little villages with small houses with tin roofs. Geraniums were pouring out of planters made out of five-liter olive oil containers. Some houses were totally whitewashed. They even whitewashed their olive oil containers making the geraniums seem an even brighter red. Grapevines created the best shade right in front of the houses. There were divans decorated with hand-embroidered pillows on the front porches. Those pillows were probably from the chest that the bride brought with her. She might have spent nights working on those delicate patterns to create a masterpiece for herself, dreaming about her future husband. Now, she was yelling at her six kids not to take the eggs from the chicken coop!

As we reached one of the few openings that led to the sea, I saw, yet again, my mother's favorite tree. She called it a "champagne glass" tree. It was really the shape of a nice champagne glass. This is one of the moments that you know how elegant my mom is. She almost belonged to a world of princesses. But she never had a day as a princess, holding a champagne glass in her white-gloved hand and talking to her prince charming, a very nice, handsome, caring gentleman.

We started to descend the mountain as the beautiful Mediterranean Sea unfolded before us. It was sparkling blue under a soft blue sky. That was your first glimpse of the Mediterranean. It was the sea that made me happy, the sea that taught me how to swim, the sea where I had my first crush, the sea where I lived my carefree days. I was bringing you with me to meet my sea. You had your first dip in the sea that day, in the crystal clear waters of the Mediterranean.

Silifke

We left the Taurus Mountains behind, and we first stopped at Mut. Mut is a reasonably large town built right at the skirts of the Taurus Mountains. It is the first town that greets you with a smile of the Mediterranean. That was where we drank the best *ayran*, the frothy ice cold yogurt drink with salt. After Mut, it was a beautiful one-hour ride down the hills to Silifke, my mom's hometown.

I have no memories of Tarsus, my birthplace. I was only three when we moved to Silifke. Silifke was built to be away from the sea to protect the land. Taşucu, the settlement of Holmi, where my grandparents lived, was right on the Mediterranean, which made it vulnerable to pirate attacks during its prosperous years. Silifke was founded by Seleucus, one of Alexander the Great's generals, in 300 B.C., ten kilometers inland to protect the city from sea attacks. It has a fort perched on top of a steep hill, like an eagle protecting its nest. The Göksu River runs through the city, dividing it in two. The stone bridge was built in 77-78 A.D. by the Roman Emperor Vespasianus and his sons, connecting the two parts of the city.

When we first moved to Silifke, my dad rented two adjacent rooms in a lovely garden of a house, which belonged to a tailor, his wife, and their two kids. Our kitchen was outside. My mom used to do the dishes squatting in front of a faucet right outside our door. The faucet was only a foot above the concrete floor. Their garden was full of flowers. The landlords were very surprised that none of us ever picked a flower from their garden. My mom always taught us to be nice and caring, and what our limits were. My mom had always the pride of being a good and honest person. We were very poor, but we never felt it. The love my mom gave us was so strong there was no need for anything else.

A few years later, we moved to our own house. My dad had our house built in Silifke. It was a single-story, very modern house for that time. We had the only house that had a service window between the dining room and the kitchen. My dad must have seen this somewhere. I loved that little window. My mom used to put all the dishes, plates, and glasses out, and I would pick them up and set the table. The house had three large bedrooms. The best part of the house was the garden: a big garden full of tomatoes, potatoes, scallions, onions, and chickpeas. We had fig, pomegranate, almond, and peach trees. My favorite was the fresh chickpeas. Those were not the dry or canned chickpeas, or garbanzo beans, you find in the grocery aisle. The plant is like a little bush with fresh green chickpeas in their own little green pods that shine like little jewels within the foliage of very fine leaves. They were so delicious. I would make my stop at these plants every ten minutes to have a couple. They even used to sell them, during summer months, in bunches at the markets. The other version of the chickpeas sold by street vendors was boiled chickpeas with cumin and salt.

We passed through Silifke but it wasn't until our trip in 2006 that we visited our old house in Silifke. Seeing it again hit me hard. I was sobbing. That beautiful house looked like a beat-up little dirty pink box with windows covered with iron bars to prevent theft. Our lush garden was turned into dry soil. And, it was not as big at all as I remembered. No one could have believed that once there was a green garden there. We walked around the garden to see if there was anything we could relate to the past. There were no trees and no plants. We hoped that someone would open the door and let us in. We dreamt about going into our bedroom and the living room where we played the "pirate" game. We could not knock on the door. I don't know why, but we did not have the courage to do it. I knew I would break down from so many memories.

Our house was next to the Silifke Elementary School. My brother, Mehmet, was in first grade and his teacher was one of my uncles, Ahmet Dayı. I was very upset that year when my brother started school and left me home all alone without a friend, so I used to climb over the school wall every time they had a break. I would stop whatever I was doing and run over to the wall and jump over to pretend that I was a pupil. But my clothes would give me away. I remember begging my mom to sew me a school uniform.

Dreadful School Uniforms

I don't know if some schools still have them, but during my parents' and my school years, it was almost impossible to get away from that dreadful elementary school uniform unless you attended a private school. All pupils had to go through this dress code torture. And it did not change from my parents' time to our time, and even later. No evolution and no revolution. No one dared to question the ugliness and the humiliation it created among the pupils. We were almost like those prisoners in their striped shirts and pants.

The uniform consisted of a black dress for girls, of course below the knee, all buttoned up either at the back or in the front. The same version was for the boys but shorter, just around the hips, with gray or black slacks. Both boys and girls had to wear this hard-starched, really-hurts-your-neck, blister-causing white collar that goes around your neck and buttons right where your Adam's apple is. The collar was a separate item since it needed to be washed, starched, and ironed every day. Most kids had two, so the moms would be cleaning one while the pupils wore the other. There was no way you could enter the school with a dirty one. Girls had to wear white or black socks or thick stockings in winter. Dark shoes were the code.

Hair had to be trimmed or neatly tied for girls, and it could not be longer than the earlobe for boys. Well, some of the boys really wished they had long earlobes when the principal would take his ugly big scissors out and cut this inverted Mohawk pattern on the boy's head. The only way to make your hair even was to have it shaved completely.

Every morning we would have a cleanliness test. We all would pull out our freshly ironed white handkerchiefs and place our hands on them, palms down. The teacher would walk around and check our nails. If you had dirty nails, and if your teacher was mean, she would ask you to turn your hand palms up with all fingers put together and she or he would slap the side of a big ruler right on your nails and finger tips.

The Flood at Our First House

This memory is still so vivid that I could not omit it from this book. One night, just a few days before a big flood, we watched a large snake make its way under our main door. It was very scary to see how it was coming towards us. My dad grabbed an ax. I didn't even know we had one. That was the first and last time I saw my dad with an ax doing something very brave. He hit the snake's head, which separated from its body, but the body was still moving. So he ended up chopping the snake in many pieces and putting them in a bag, which he buried on the other side of the dirt road. When the big flood hit the next day and unearthed everything, I was so scared that those wiggling snake pieces would invade our house!

It was springtime. The large river, Göksu, meaning "green water," was running wild after days and days of endless rain. Göksu is the river where the Emperor Frederick Barbarossa was drowned during the Third Crusade in 1190. My dad still picks on my mom, questioning whether her ancestors had some interaction with the crusaders since my mom has very fair skin and hazel eyes. She definitely did not have the look of a Mediterranean native. Sakallı Dede had blue eyes and blond hair. So much for the Mediterranean blood I carry in me!

That day I had one *kuruş*, the smallest monetary unit in Turkey, in my pocket. It is just like a cent is to a dollar. One hundred *kuruş* makes one Turkish *lira*. At that time *kuruş* was becoming so rare that finding one was like a treasure hunt for us. After the rain, while playing outside, I dropped my *kuruş* into a puddle. I searched and searched, but the puddle was pretty big. I looked around, puddles were everywhere. Then I saw it coming; the river was overflowing its bed, rushing through the streets and houses. In almost no time, the entire neighborhood was under water, except for our house. Our house was on higher ground than the others. Maybe my dad knew that this could happen; you know how smart he is. Not only did he have the house built on higher ground, he also had the foundation raised about seven or eight steps. The water reached the last step. My father started, with the help of all our neighbors, fleeing to our house, hanging all our valuables on hinges from the ceiling. Our refrigerator was dangling from the ceiling in the middle of our living room. I don't remember how long the flood lasted, but I remember vividly my family and the neighbors on the roof with a helicopter hovering above us, and my dearest grandfather, Kara Dede, was shouting from the helicopter, "Is everyone OK? Do you want us to come by boats to rescue you?" They dropped us bread, feta cheese, and water. I still wonder if he was serious about the boats. But I know he was capable of doing everything for us. Somehow he got the military helicopter to take him to check on his family. He could have even had the boats carried from the sea to save us. The water slowly receded, leaving a thick layer of mud for all the neighbors to clean up.

I am sure my parents were worried that time. But for me, it was an amazing adventure. I had that adrenaline rush. Still today, I get excited when I hear any wild weather predictions, either snow or rain, and wait excitedly for the approach of a big storm. The power amazes me, and I feel like I am the brave warrior ready to take it on. Kind of stupid, I guess, but that is me.

A Few More Silifke Memories

I do not remember much about Silifke, but there are a few more memories I can tell you about. Most of them were during our two-year stay at our new house in Silifke before we moved to Ankara.

My neighbor's sheep had given birth to a stark white lamb with beautiful black eyes, like two pieces of coal in snow. It became my pet. I loved running with him. With my ponytail flying in the air, he would hop next to me. He followed me everywhere. I tied a red ribbon around his neck. We became inseparable. Every night, before going to bed, I would take him back to his mother.

One day, my mom left the kitchen door open. My little lamb followed me into the kitchen and devoured a large pot of rice, part of our dinner. My parents still laugh about this event. My mom never yelled at me or even came close to being angry with me. I suspect that she probably told me that it was a funny thing but I should be more careful, and cooked another pot of rice right away before my dad came home.

We three siblings, being very close in age, used to play together almost every day. We would use all the chairs and couches in the living room and use sheets to make a house. Or we would pull two chairs face to face to make a pirate's ship. I was always the little victim who would be kidnapped. Being the youngest, I had to live with these treatments. I would be tied to a corner of a chair, the stern of the ship, until I was rescued by the savior, one of my siblings. My siblings would fight for me while I watched them with excitement and cheer for the day's designated "hero."

I got my first scar in our Silifke house. While playing catch from one room to another, I stepped on the hot iron and burned the back of my foot badly. There is still a tiny scar left there.

There were, unfortunately, mice all around the house. Traps could not keep up with them. Finally, my father discovered the nest filled with almost transparent baby mice underneath the wooden floor of one of our bedrooms. That was the end of the mouse infestation in our house. We were happy that they were destroyed, even though they looked cute. My brother was the only one who had developed a phobia, especially after the horrible incident he had. One night in his dream, he thought he was playing with a "cotton ball" and kept squeezing. We all woke up with his scream. He was squeezing a mouse!

Three of us slept in the same room until my brother reached eleven. After that, my sister and I shared a room until she got married. My brother had his own room, the tiniest one in the house. But at least he had a room of his own.

My mom used to make us take afternoon naps until I was about seven years old. We hated that. My mom would scare us by holding a frying pan or a rolling pin, a traditional very long thin one, in her hand standing by the door until we fell asleep. We would not even dare to open our eyes. We would then drift into a nice afternoon nap. I wonder what she would have done if we had gotten up and tried to run out of the room. I bet she would not have been able to do anything. The real reason for us to accept the fact that we had to sleep was we loved her so much that we did not want her feel badly that she failed to get us to sleep. Anything she asked from us, we did. She never forced anything on us, and she was never a demanding mom.

Taşucu

After leaving Silifke, we turned right and drove towards Taşucu. My heart was pounding again, as it always does whenever I leave Silifke to go to Taşucu. I knew that this was going to be sad. We no longer had our stone house. My grandmother was already gone. Memories from my childhood and my teenage years will not be as vivid as before. I was there every summer for twenty some years. No more. There was a new chapter in our lives now.

I loved going to Taşucu every summer for three months and every winter for two weeks during our school breaks in February. I would leave the day school closed, and come back a few days before school opened. My grandparents' house had a beautiful garden with tall stone walls. From outside, you could only see part of the second floor and the tree tops. There was a stable to the left of the garden door entrance, where our donkey resided, sometimes sharing his residency with a few chickens. The entry door to the garden, to our poor-man's "estate," was a double wooden door, very old, falling apart, with holes in it, but still functioning. It probably needed a good painting in the past 100 years. It had a big iron key hole and a latch.

When you opened the door, you would immediately be on a path of hardened soil lined with pomegranate trees, with beautiful orange-red flowers in summer and juicy fruits in the fall. A couple of these trees bore a sour version of the fruit. We used to shake the kernels of these with salt in a bowl and eat them.

To the right of the trees, there was a big garden with mature lemon, olive, and orange trees. And there were all sorts of wild grasses among the trees where we would have our imagination run wild and feel that it was a prairie. In the middle of this garden, there stood a giant stone wheel, all one piece, and maybe about five-feet high. The stone was perched on a grooved round grinding stone bed. There was a tree trunk serving as a lever to turn the stone wheel around to crush the olives on the stone bed. The only power we had to do this was one "donkey-power." This is where my grandmother would crush the olives from our olive orchard to make cold-pressed extra virgin olive oil.

When you walked down the path, you would come to a concrete landing area large enough to put a large divan, and an extended porch for a table and a few chairs. At one end of the landing there was a faucet, our only water intake for the entire house, only a foot above the ground. There we washed our dishes, tied the hose to wash the landing, watered the garden, and took showers in the summer. In winter we used the storage room as a bath house.

When you faced the house, on the left there was a small pool to wash olives before they were crushed and layers of little stone pools that allowed olive oil to drip from pool to pool. There was a vegetable garden right after that and remains of another stone house, where we played for days and days pretending to be grownups. My grandmother had a large tomato patch and a vegetable garden filled with cucumbers, eggplants, garlic, scallions, parsley, squash, and some other vegetables.

At the back of the house was a large back yard with two olive trees infested with bee hives. The bees would chase us constantly, and it was a game for us to irritate them and run away as fast as we could. There were enormous cactus trees bearing an abundance of cactus fruit (also called prickly pear) on hot summer days. All summer long, my Kara Dede would pick about fifty of them before the sun was up when they were still cool, and peel them as if they were the most delicate objects. It was great to watch him peel the fruit. He would hold a fork and a knife in his big hands. Without touching the cactus fruit, he would make three cutting motions and the juicy pear would come out. Here is the rule on how you peel this fruit. The goal is not to get those pricks on your fingers, so you use a fork and a knife. You hold the pear down with the fork and cut the ends of the pear, and slit the skin and peel it with one motion.

He would put the pears in the refrigerator so that they would be ice cold when we returned from our morning swim. Ah! The Mediterranean early in the morning. All my summers, around seven in the morning, after breakfast, I would take my towel to go to the beach. Cool sand under my feet, lemonade air, and water soft and gray blue. Nobody was yet on the beach. I would walk into the water very slowly instead of plunging in. It was never cold. You really did not need to worry about jumping in to get over the first shock of cold water. I would walk and watch my toes disturbing the ripples of sand formations at the bottom and little fish swimming away. Not a single object was in the water except fish and sea shells. The water was so clean you could see everything in it.

I would swim to the breakwater a few hundred meters away and still see the bottom of the sea and the rippled sand that I could no longer disturb with my toes and the shimmering sunlight swirling around the ripples. The sea would stay calm for a couple of hours. We used to call that morning look of the Mediterranean "like a linen sheet." Not a single ripple. Only a slight "whoosh" sound when tiny two-inch waves broke on the white soft sand. You would swim very softly so as not to disturb the sea and the amazing healing that stillness gave you. I will never forget the water sound my arms would make while swimming softly—the best Zen music on earth.

Around ten in the morning the beach crowds would start coming in with their sand chairs, umbrellas, towels, coolers, radios, and everything else they could take from home. The morning peace would cease, and the daily summer beach time would start. I would usually stay another hour, make plans with my friends for the afternoon, and then walk back home. I would take my shower; actually hose myself down under the date tree. The water in the hose was usually hot at first since it was in the sun all morning, and then would get cooler as the minutes passed. I loved the change in the water temperature. That was my daily wash. Then twice a week I would wash myself with shampoo and soap in our storage room in a makeshift bath. Swimming in the Mediterranean gives you great benefits. Even if you sweat, you never stink from all that salt on your skin. You become one of those preserved fish with lots of salt. Bacalao, anyone?

Since my grandparents always woke up around four in the morning, my grandmother would wake us up at six, yelling at us that it was already lunch time. I still wake up very early. I learned to love the quietness and peacefulness of the morning.

Our breakfast usually consisted of *bazlama*, honey, olives, feta cheese, *kaşar* cheese, yogurt, butter, tomatoes, and cucumber. Not all of them at one time, but a combination of two or three together.

The evenings at Taşucu evolved with my age. When we were kids, during hot summer nights, when staying in the house became unbearable, all the Taşucu inhabitants—moms, dads, kids, dogs, and cats—would go to the pier to cool down and get away from mosquitoes. The heat would still be unbearable in the evenings. The mosquitoes would arrive around eight or nine at night and stay active until morning. The worst hours were until about two in the morning. They would sting whatever part of your body they could get. You had to sleep under the mosquito net set up above your bed, but when the weather was hot, these tents would make breathing even more impossible. So life in Taşucu became very active after dark. The families would spread their cotton blankets on the concrete pier. Some would bring a radio or a cassette player. Women would bring their needlework. The vendors, usually kids carrying baskets full of goods, would yell, selling corn, sunflower seeds, flavored snow cones, boiled chickpeas with cumin, soda, water, candy, and gum. Families would interact while the kids were playing. Like ants, we would create mounds of sunflower seed shells. Kids and men would fish off the pier. The bait was usually bread dough made at home. Around midnight, when the air was cooling down, the kids would start to drift off to sleep. I remember my Kara Dede carrying me on his back. Sometimes I would wake up and could walk at that point, but I always pretended that I was still asleep. I enjoyed being carried on his back. It was a great feeling to have him being the best and the tallest grandfather on earth. When we came home, he would put me in bed, and he would then sleep face down with his money in his front pocket and start snoring immediately. He literally would start snoring as soon as his head hit the pillow. The rest of the family would hunt down a few mosquitoes before they went to sleep.

My brother and I loved going fishing early—at about four in the morning. We would take our fishing lines and the dough that my grandmother made for us. We would sit next to each other on the pier and dangle our fishing lines. There were no fishing rods at that time. Our middle and index fingers were the rods, holding the fishing line, waiting for that exciting moment of the "fish bite." In about an hour, we would watch the magnificent sun rise over the horizon and would walk back home to have breakfast and go swimming. Some of those mornings we caught enough fish to feed all of us for lunch and dinner.

My days in Taşucu were simple, yet relaxing. I was most fascinated by how clean and blue the sea was and how comfortable it was to interact with the locals. I knew everybody in the town. On all my arrivals to Taşucu early in the morning, my grandfather would hold my arm and we would walk on the main street, the only real street that cars went through. He would proudly show me off.

Once in a while, I went fishing with the most colorful fisherman in town, Nail (pronounced na-ill) Abi. He was not a "nail." Remember these are Turkish names. He was tall, slim, with dark curly hair and dark brown eyes. A very typical Turkish Mediterranean look. He was very close to our family. Almost every week he would bring freshly caught fish to my grandmother. After our fishing trips, I would walk with him to the local restaurants to distribute fresh fish for lunch and dinner.

I never carried money in Taşucu. Whichever store I went to, whichever restaurant I ate in, and whichever coffee house I drank Turkish tea in, I would tell them to write it to my grandfather's account. And he would pay them daily whenever he passed those places. The amount was nothing compared to his daily spending.

Winter in Taşucu

Lasting only two months, the winters in Taşucu had their own charm, as endless rains collected enough water to last through cloudless summers, and the Taurus Mountains got their hefty share of snow. The winters were as cozy as you can imagine. I never spent the entire winter there after we moved to Ankara, but did spend the first two weeks of February when we had our winter breaks. Since we did not celebrate Christmas, and had only two days off during the New Year, the schools would get two weeks off in February. I would take a bus the day my school entered the winter break and go to see my grandparents, escaping from my father's anger to their cozy arms.

The bus usually took about eight hours, and cost almost nothing. My father would give me a few liras, enough for my travel, and relied on my grandfather to take care of me. I was not a big spender anyway. Who needs money when you visit Kara Dede! The bus would go through a famous opening, Gülek Boğazı, in the Taurus Mountains. These mountains stretch from one end to the other of the Turkish Mediterranean coastline, separating the middle Anatolia from the warm Mediterranean climate. The snow on the mountains usually reached about four or five feet high. The snow would sparkle under the moonlight with delicate mounds and curves created by the howling wind.

After passing the Gülek Boğazı, the weather would immediately get warmer, the snow would disappear, and the landscape would change. The pine trees would give way to fruit trees and vineyards. The grass was as green as it gets, and wild flowers sprouted everywhere, especially stark-white daisies. The almond trees would be in full blossom with their white delicate flowers with a touch of pink. A few bus stop areas would offer *tost* (fresh panini toast with cheese) and *ayran* at three in the morning. You really would not need a winter jacket after that point. A windbreaker and a light sweater would do fine.

I would arrive at Silifke around five in the morning and would take a minibus to Taşucu, which was only ten kilometers away. The closer we came to Taşucu the smell of the sea would greet you. I would find my Kara

Dede in the local coffee house playing cards. He immediately would fold his hand and leave the table. None of his gambling friends would object. We would walk home together, and my grandmother would be waiting for me anxiously. She would have the wood-burning stove right in the middle of our kitchen, which also served as our sitting room. I would have my breakfast—homemade cheese, yogurt, and my grandmother's bread. Kara Dede would roast chestnuts on the stove every night. The two large rooms downstairs were the main rooms used in the house. One room served as a kitchen plus sitting room, the other room as our bedroom and also our second sitting room. There were three large divans encircling the three walls of the bedroom. We would all sleep on these divans at night with just sheets covering the divan and a few light cotton covers in summer, and comforters in winter. Our pillows and covers would be piled up in a corner during the day. We usually had tenants upstairs, so except for visiting their rooms, I hardly have memories about the second floor.

While roasting chestnuts, Kara Dede would tell us stories from his childhood. Sometimes the villagers would bring wild mushrooms and game meat, and we would cook them outside on a makeshift grill consisting of a wood fire and a metal grid. We would eat the food right there by the fire, trying not to burn our fingers. Those were tasty morsels. Imagine hot grilled mushrooms sprinkled with sea salt! In winter I took long walks by the sea, which was sometimes calm and sometimes raging with storms.

My leisure times in Taşucu changed as I changed from a little girl to a teenager. I continued to hang out with my grandfather, but I started to spend more time with my friends. I hardly stayed home, especially in the summer. I spent every day swimming, snorkeling, catching octopus, grilling it on coal, drinking wine and beer on the beach, and swimming under the moonlight with my friends. There were eighteen of us. Those carefree days with lots of love still bring a smile to my face. I loved those times, and I hope you live such times with your family.

Yayla: Our Summer Place in the Taurus Mountains

The day after our arrival at Taşucu, we took a tour of our relatives' houses. Now it was my time to show off my beautiful baby. I had not seen my relatives for many years and it was so homey to be greeted as if time had stopped years ago and we just turned the clocks on again. You were blond with hazel eyes, another non-Mediterranean looking member of our family. One of my cousins wanted to send his wife with me to America so that their kids would be as beautiful as you are. They were joking that the waters in America must have done some magic. Wonderful people. I love them all.

Now it was time to introduce you to our *yayla* up on the Taurus Mountains. We drove again, climbing up the Taurus Mountains, with Taşucu getting smaller and smaller, and we finally reached Boklalan.

In the warmer areas of Turkey, *yayla* is a place people usually would go during hot summer months. These are villages that are perched high in the mountains. In the old times, the benefits and the beauty of spending time at the beach was not at all heard of. My grandfather would rent a truck and all the necessities needed in *yayla* would be piled high on the bed of the truck, including us. We had cotton mattresses, linens, pots, pans, food, clothes, cats, a donkey, and chickens. In the old times, as my grandparents used to tell us, they would go to *yayla* via a mountain path on a donkey. They would have a lantern to keep the wolves away and would travel all night to arrive in the morning. For us, with the truck, it was only an hour. I learned just a few months ago that the mountain they were traveling through was actually one giant marble. Now, it is a marble quarry. It looks like a marble cake half-bitten by a giant wolf.

Our *yayla* house was in Boklalan, high up the marble mountain, shortened from *Boklu Alan*, meaning "field with poop" or "poopy field." I don't know why and where the name comes from. I assume it used to be a grazing field for cows. When the founder of Turkey, Atatürk, visited Boklalan in the 1920s, he changed its name to Cumhuriyet Alanı, meaning "the field of the republic." There were only a few houses there. We all knew each other and visited each other. Each house had a small vineyard for making grape molasses and the raisins for the winter months and for our daily eating during the summer. We had a two-room stone structure, and the rooms shared a wall in between. The entries to these two rooms were separate. The shade in front of the entrances was from dry tree branches put on a wooden frame. There were no doors, no windows, not even window frames, just openings that looked like big holes. To prevent us from getting bitten by snakes, scorpions, and centipedes, we always slept under a mosquito net. The beds were just cotton mattresses placed on jute rugs, on the hardened dry mud floor, to keep the moisture away. The mattresses were placed side by side so we would all cuddle up together and sleep. There was no electricity. Only the fire from the hearth on cold nights and maybe a gas lamplight would give a glowing flicker on the walls.

We had an outhouse for a bathroom, a hole and two planks and walls made out of oak branches for privacy. If we needed to go during the night, adults would let the kids go on the side of the house since they were afraid we would fall into the hole in the pitch dark, or a jackal would wander near the outhouse. Some nights I would wake up and listen to the animals outside—maybe the sliding of a snake by our bed or jackals at a distance. Somehow, I was not scared. I guess if you grow up in that environment you never develop a fear for such things. But being away for so long and being used to the comfort of a house with real doors and windows, I don't think I would be able to sleep there easily today. My grandfather sold the place anyway, just like everything else he owned.

During the day, our best times were going with our grandmother to chop wood and carry the branches home. She would take all three of us while my mom cooked lunch. She would carry the big ax that I was always afraid of. She would choose old, dying trees and start chopping the branches down. We would pick shiny mineral rocks. If she was in a good mood, she would make us a swing by tying a thick rope over a high branch. When she finished chopping wood, she would prepare bundles for everyone's size, with the heaviest load on her. We would line up by the side of the main road, a dirt road, follow her footsteps, and walk back home. Another great pastime I remember was picking grapes from the vines, washing them right there, and eating the sun-drenched delicious grapes. My favorite was champagne grapes. I loved the bursting of little grapes in my mouth. That is one of your favorites too. I guess I caused that, buying them every time I see them in our local fresh produce store.

My mother and my grandmother would go near the creek to wash our clothes, the old-fashioned way, by stomping and pounding the laundry on rocks. My dad and grandfather were rarely with us. My dad gave summer courses to earn extra money, and gambled some. My grandfather stayed in Taşucu and dealt with trading tomatoes and olives, and gambled some. He would hire pickers and arrange with the landowners to have their crops picked and shipped to the big cities. My dad and my Kara Dede would come over on the weekends. It was such a joy to see them getting off a truck, with my grandfather carrying saçks of watermelons, melons, almonds, walnuts, and other goodies. He would bring his grandchildren some cheap plastic toys and candy. We would look forward to their arrival on weekends. Not really my father's, but definitely my grandfather's.

Some days we would walk to the nearest village to one of my uncles' homes. There was a path that would wind around the pine trees. There were *hayıt* bushes (chaste tree) everywhere, a kind of butterfly bush, in full bloom with purple and white flowers. The smell of *hayıt* always reminds me of those days.

Sometimes in the summer we would take a bus to another *yayla*, Gökbelen, almost the size of a big village, on higher grounds. The town center was around a mosque, surrounded by tall walnut trees. Our fingers would turn black from eating fresh walnuts. There were butchers grilling lamb chops right in front of their shops, with wooden tables and chairs spread around a creek. We would sit under the shade of a walnut tree and eat our lamb chops in cool weather. At the houses we visited, they would serve *sıkma*. *Sıkma* is made by filling *bazlama* with feta cheese, onions, and parsley. After you wrap the hot *bazlama* around the filling you need to squeeze it with your hands, almost leaving imprints of your fingers on it to warm up the fillings. The heat would penetrate the cheese and melt it. Or we would eat *gözleme*, thin dough crepes filled with spinach or cheese and cooked on a *saç*. We would drink *ayran*. It tasted exactly like kefir. The foam of *ayran* would fill half of our glasses, just like beer, and leave a white mustache every time you took a sip. We had an abundance of fruit and nuts—apples, pears, plums, grapes, black and white mulberries, almonds, walnuts, and pistachios.

One of my memories of Boklalan is related to my first and only doll. During the summer of 1963, my father went to the United States to study modern mathematics for three months. He was one of the few teachers chosen from Turkey. Later he became the teacher of the teachers, teaching modern mathematics to all mathematics teachers in Turkey. This gave our family a chance to travel to many parts of Turkey every summer for many years. He was one of the five best modern math teachers in the country, and I was a proud high school student showing off my dad's high school mathematics book as the adopted textbook in Turkey's public school system.

When my father came back from America, we were still in Boklalan. I was six years old. He got off the bus with two large suitcases and a big doll in his arms. The doll was the size of a two-year-old. He said this was for me. He said he bought it in Florida. I named my doll Florida and played with her for many years to come. Later, my sister's daughter Derya played with her too. I learned how to knit and sew while making clothes for my doll. Florida was always with me, just like you and Donald Ducky. Donald Ducky was your stuffed puppet. You could put your hand in the opening and use your fingers to move his beak and arms. You loved Donald Ducky; he traveled with you around the world. It was stolen once at the hotel where we stayed in Cazumel. You cried, so heart-broken that all the hotel personnel went looking for it. Somehow, Donald Ducky showed up on your bed the next day. It is still in your room, a bit beaten and chewed by our dog Tornado, but happy to be your favorite stuffed animal.

Can you imagine what my father would be thinking, comparing his three months in the United States flying on airplanes, staying in plush hotel rooms, eating at fancy restaurants, and coming back to Boklalan to a two-room something with no window frames! I don't remember him mentioning anything to us. But somehow he stopped eating egg whites for a few years. Maybe it was the fad during his visit to the United States. Whatever happened, my dad's new position changed our lives forever. That was the mark of ending my life as a small town girl with a free-style nature and the beginning of my life as a city girl in a scary big city, Ankara, the capital of Turkey. That was also the year I started the first grade.

I could not recognize Boklalan when we arrived after all those years. We stopped our car right in front of where we used to live. It was sad to see that our little shack was gone, replaced by a villa. But the garden was the same. My own champagne grapes, hanging from a 100-year-old grapevine, were still there. So was the plum tree we used to climb. The garden seemed really small. When I was little, I thought we had a very big garden. The tiny orchard, as I remembered, consisted of only about ten grapevines. The new owners let us walk around the garden. The years that we spent our summers there felt like a million years ago. I was a little blonde girl, wearing a cotton summer dress, with my shoes on the wrong feet, running like a duckling.

Çınarcık

It was time to say goodbye, just for now, to our relatives and to Kara Dede, and to go north where my parents had a summer house near İstanbul.

With my dad's lump-sum retirement money, my parents bought a summer place in Çınarcık, a small two-bedroom apartment a few hundred yards from the Marmara Sea. We only had a sliver of the sea view between the two apartment buildings in front of us. It was not at all like Taşucu, but it had its own charms. Çınarcık was an old resort town of İstanbul where the upper middle class had apartment flats so that the wives and children could spend time in Çınarcık while the husbands worked during the week in İstanbul. There was a daily ferry service between Çınarcık and İstanbul. On Friday evenings, the ferry would arrive full to capacity, bringing the husbands home for the weekend. The wives would have the *rakı* table ready by the beach for the husbands. There would be a bonfire going alongside the coal grill to grill tender lamb chops, *köfte* (spiced meatballs), and shish kebabs. The coal from the bonfire would feed the coal grill for late-night grilling. The men would drink their milk-colored *rakı* (when you mix *rakı* with water, it turns white). There would be *çoban salatası* (peasant salad: finely chopped tomatoes, cucumbers, peppers, onions, parsley, and mint mixed with olive oil, lemon, and salt), feta cheese, slices of melon, and bread. Husbands and wives would sit around the wooden tables on wobbly wooden chairs until past midnight. Their conversations about kids, politics, and life would turn into singing—mostly sad bellowing songs. The teenagers would be on their own, walking to town for ice cream or soda. The younger ones would hang out around their parents, playing with the sand on the beach or swimming in the sea. Many of them would still be in their bathing suits. The town center was always lively with small kebab restaurants and some open-air taverns with live music, some even with belly dancing. Some nights it would get so crowded that we used to call it a human traffic jam. Actually, about ten years ago, there was literally a human gridlock in downtown Bodrum, one of the most popular resort towns in Turkey. They had to bring extra police in to guide the crowd to untangle Bodrum's downtown.

The mornings of Çınarcık were absolutely the opposite. My parents owned that apartment in Çınarcık for more than twenty-five years, until my mom got Parkinson's disease, and she walked every morning during the three months of summer. She would get up at seven in the morning and gather any neighbor she could wake up. They would walk to the town center. It was about a twenty- or thirty-minute walk depending on the pace of that day's walkers. Since Çınarcık was a bit upper middle class place, you would see women wearing shiny white sneakers and matching velour warm-up suits with sequins on them, rarely used except on these Çınarcık walks. I loved joining those walks. Even you joined us, when you were just a baby. I would put you in your stroller, and with my mom, my sister, and the neighbors, we would walk on the sidewalk right next to the beach, which would take us to the town center. Çınarcık was built on a crescent-shaped beach with hills rising right beyond the apartments. Two roads, each one-way, connected the entire town. All apartments were built around these two roads. The sidewalk was pretty wide all the way to the town center. We would listen to the gentle waves, watching the sea color change from gray to blue as the sun rose. Right at the town center there would be villagers selling their fresh produce and fishermen selling their overnight catch. The fishermen would carry fish from the boats they pulled right onto the beach. The seagulls would circle above us, hoping to get the innards of the fish. There was no worry about whether the fish was fresh or not; some of them would be still wiggling. We would order our fish, and while it was being cleaned, we would buy bread from the bakery, yogurt from the dairy, and a newspaper from the stand. The best part was to walk around the villagers with their produce spread onto the sidewalks. Imagine choosing the best tomatoes with their intoxicating smell from the sun, parsley, mint, fresh garlic, scallions, beans, mulberries, blackberries, carrots, grapes, figs, pears, peaches the size of a small melon—you name it. We would take a break at a tea shop on the way home, and have our first morning tea feeling the sun heat our arms and legs. Before you were born we, all women, would fight over who would carry the heaviest load on the way home. Your stroller helped the entire walking team for about two or three years. We would hang as much as possible on your stroller's handles. I remember once stopping to take a breather and letting the stroller's handles go, and watched you and the stroller fall backwards.

The great earthquake of the Marmara region in 1999 took a significant toll on Çınarcık life. My parents lost some relatives. Our place was unharmed. But many people, including my dad, sold their places in the next few years.

We really had a good time there. The best pastimes were breakfasts and afternoon tea times.

Ankara Homes

Although I have better memories of Taşucu and Çınarcık, Ankara homes were the ones where I spent most of my time in Turkey.

After my father successfully completed his three months of modern mathematics education in the United States, he was appointed to be a mathematics teacher at Ankara Fen Lisesi (Ankara Science High School), at that time the most prestigious free boarding high school in the country. There were great boarding schools in İstanbul already. However, they were mostly for the rich and the privileged who happened to have smart kids and lots of money. The students were selected to enter Fen Lisesi after a very tough two sets of entry tests. From the thousands who took these tests, only seventy-five of the brightest would be selected. My brother made it. I failed on the second test. But later in the university entry exams, I beat him.

During the end of the summer of 1963, we moved to Ankara. That is when my life in a big city began. It was a memorable move. We had all our belongings piled up high on a truck. The truck driver, Kara Dede, my mom, my dad, my brother, and I were in the front seat lined up like sardines. I was on my mom's lap, and my brother was on my dad's. I spent the entire trip sleeping in my mom's arms until we reached Ankara. Since there was not enough space for everyone in the front, my grandmother and my sister were at the back of the truck lying in between layers of rugs under the covers. Of course, there was a limitation on how many people and household items a truck could carry, so they were in hiding in case there was a control at a police or military checkpoint. It was a year in which Turkey had a military coup, something that happened every ten years or so. There was a curfew in the big cities until six in the morning. When we reached the outskirts of Ankara, the military police stopped us and we were held there for a few hours until the night curfew was over. My sister and my grandmother were as quiet as mice in the back and could not even move for about two hours.

After six in the morning, our life in Ankara started—living in apartments, watching the roads while crossing, noise, cars, and attending large schools where the teachers were not your close relatives or family friends. That was a new era for my entire family. We took some years to adjust, but my heart never left my past. The smell of the Mediterranean, the crackling fire, rain, the outhouse, stone houses, jasmine, bougainvillea, cactus pear, pomegranates, olives, grapes, and everything else about Mediterranean food and colors take me back to the most important years of my life.

Moving from a small town to a big city has a big impact on any person, but especially on kids. We found the new world to be very scary. Even the language felt different. Coming from the south, we sometimes had different words for objects. We were afraid to speak for fear of being picked on.

Ankara is on a high plateau, and you quickly discover how cold the winter gets. We saw our first snow the first winter we were in Ankara. I remember having trouble walking in the snow. We were delighted that they closed the schools when there was heavy snow. On our days off we would use my mom's baking trays to slide down the little hills near our apartment. For us, before moving to Ankara, snow was an ingredient of a delicious desert. People would bring it from the Taurus Mountains in a basket, freshly packed, and we would pour grape molasses over it and eat it like ice cream. In Ankara the snow was everywhere, and it was not as white and clean as the snow on Taurus Mountains. Just a few hours after hitting the ground, with the heavy pollution in Ankara at that time, the snow would turn gray. At least it cleared the coal dust in the air. Today Ankara is a much cleaner city, thanks to the city-wide enforced natural gas heating instead of coal heating and to an abundance of green parks built over the years.

I had my first scare of the happenings in a big city where trust takes different dimensions. The year we moved to Ankara a little girl was kidnapped and was never found. It was the first time this kind of kidnapping happened. Parents warned their kids every day not to talk to strangers. It was no more a little Mediterranean town; we needed to be more careful. And my parents' advice worked one time. I was walking home from school. A man, unshaven with dirty clothes, approached me and asked me if I wanted candy. Without looking back, I ran all the way home with my little skinny legs. I rang the bell with my legs trembling and jumped into my mom's arms. I was terrified. I could not imagine not seeing my mother ever again.

Another terrifying event the same year was when I almost choked on a piece of apple. I only remember one of my dad's friends holding me from my feet, upside down, and shaking me and hitting me on my back. The same year, the same friend gave me a glass full of orange juice and asked me to drink it. He was having fun giving me vodka with orange juice and watching me get silly afterwards. It was probably hilarious for them, but I was pretty sick the next day. Years later, my brother and I played a similar trick on a two-year-old boy, not with vodka but beer. Poor kid, he was bouncing from wall to wall, slurring, with a silly smile on his face. And I almost peed in my pants from laughter.

We moved three times before we bought an apartment flat in 1968. Our first apartment was in Yenimahalle. We were there one year. At that time it was one of the new districts far away from the city center and one of the most affordable ones. We lived in Cebeci one year, and three years in Bahçelievler on First Avenue. Then we bought our first apartment flat on Sixth Street, just one street down from First Avenue. Three years later, in 1970, we had to move to Kızılay, the center of Ankara, and lived there until my parents sold that apartment in 2000. Now they live in Çayyolu, one of the expanding regions of Ankara, in a very cute two-bedroom apartment. Every Saturday, when I am visiting, I watch the bazaar set up early in the morning from their living room window. As the day progresses, I stay by the window, listening to the bustling sound of the merchants and watching the colorful fresh produce disappearing into the bags of shoppers.

The apartment in Yenimahalle was spacious. It had three large bedrooms and one small room. Since we three siblings were still sharing a room, the third bedroom was a guest room, plus it hosted my mom's sewing machine. For many years she made our clothes, including our underwear, to save every penny my dad made with his little teaching salary. The tiny fourth room was our cat's bedroom. We found her on our door step one night. We heard the little meow sounds and opened the door to find this little kitten. She stayed with us until she grew up. We took her to our grandparents so that she could have the freedom of running outside, or that is what our parents told us. Maybe the real story was that they had it with the cat and they had to make up this story so that we would believe that this was something good for our cat. She was a very independent cat, and she took off one day from my grandparents' house and never returned. Her name was Sarman, named after a character in a poem that I had to memorize in first grade.

After the first year of struggling to adjust to city life, with little money, we three siblings ended up growing up in Ankara and loving it.

I had never been in a high-rise building until we moved to our apartment in Cebeci. We not only moved horizontally from the outskirts to the very center of Ankara, we also moved vertically from the first floor to the tenth. There was a balcony in the living room overlooking the Atatürk Boulevard, one of the main avenues in Ankara. The day we moved in, I walked up to the balcony to see what was out there, immediately getting on all fours, petrified to go closer to the railing. I still remember the butterflies in my stomach. I was on my knees for about three months, until I got used to the height.

That is the year my brother developed sleepwalking. He would sit up straight in bed and start his commentary on soccer games (he is a crazy fanatic soccer fan!) in his sleep. One night, my dad woke up to find our front door wide open. He checked the apartment for a possible intruder, and ended up finding my brother's bed empty. He ran down the ten flights of stairs (the building elevator hardly ever worked). He found my brother on the sidewalk of the boulevard, strolling down the street in his pajamas, still asleep. After that night, my dad placed bolts on the top of the entry door where my brother could not reach.

I must have been eight when my parents started leaving us alone in the house so they could go out and visit their friends. My sister was only eleven and she was in charge as the oldest! Our parents were not the only ones leaving their young kids home alone. We would wait for our parents to come home, all cuddled together and listening to every strange sound. We would read books to each other. I still remember those little thin books that my mom used to buy for about a penny each. They were about two detectives solving mysteries.

It is very common in Turkey to call family or friends and tell them you would like to visit them. It could be that evening or another day. These visits were usually after-dinner visits, starting around nine at night. Visitors would stay until about eleven or twelve. You would sit around the living room and talk about nearly everything. The host would serve tea and baked goods, usually one salty and one sweet. Many moms exchanged recipes on these visits. My mom had pieces of papers with recipes on them. All the recipes had their own names, such as Suzan's almond cookie or Yüksel's *börek*. Here in the United States, I still do the same thing, just collecting recipes from my friends and food magazines. I have a pile of recipes the same way my mom did.

Our cousin Metin Abi, my dad's nephew, lived with us until he went to college. He moved to the dorms during college years, and years later I learned the reason for his leaving. My dad thought my sister was growing up, just eleven years old(!), and it would not be a good idea to have a college kid in the house. He was a big brother to us, and we felt safe when he was with us on those lonely, scary nights when our parents were out. However, another thing I learned years later was that my grandmother thought that it would be best to have my father give my sister to his nephew as his wife.

The old minds always think to keep the family to themselves. The irony is Metin Abi died a few months after Güngör Abi.

Sometimes our parents would take us on their visits. We loved to read magazines for hours during these visits. The hosts always commented on how great we were. "The kids are no trouble," they would say. Actually we were hungry for reading about everything, since my parents hardly purchased books and magazines. We loved to go with my parents, especially if the host had kids our age. They always had cooler toys than ours. I always liked the Legos. I used to build all kinds of houses with them.

After Cebeci, we moved to Bahçelievler. The first three years in Bahçelievler we lived on First Avenue. My dad started to make some money by giving private lessons at the tutoring centers. And, with an invitation from the government, he and two of his colleagues from the Fen Lisesi, that prestigious high school, started to write mathematics books for high school students. These books were the textbooks for high school students for the entire country. Of course, they received only a little money from the government, for being the authors, but not from the sales of the books. I remember seeing my name on the math problems. Think about it! The problem starts: "Nuray wanted to buy a dozen eggs . . . ."

Imagine, the math book you used in your high school was written by your dad. I was quite popular in high school, both among students and teachers. That gave me a big boost to pull all A's in all my classes. I had one D in freshman year, and every other grade was an A. The D was from my physical education class, because I could not do a somersault on the horse vault. I would end up landing on my face every time I tried. My gym teacher was very sorry afterwards, but it was too late for her to change my grade. To make up for my inability in any sport, I signed up for the high school dance team. The team represented the high school at national holiday events at the Ankara stadium. After that, it did not matter what I did in gym, I got an A.

We lived in two places in Bahçelievler and both were heaven for teenagers. The first apartment building on First Avenue had about ten or eleven kids very close in age. During summer months, we would play outside until two in the morning. One of the kids would act as Dracula and would chase us all night long. During the day, we had typical kids' play. The entry to the apartment building was concrete with a diamond pattern, and we would play hopscotch there. Just last year I went with my sister to visit our close relative still living there, and all my memories came back. My sister and I did the hopscotch game again. I looked at the back yard; the same plum tree, just slightly bigger, was still there. We lived there for three years until we bought our first apartment in Ankara with the money from the sale of our house in Silifke. It was on Sixth Street and only a block away from First Avenue. There were about twenty-five kids in the building on Sixth Street. Each family had at least three kids; some had four. We were a great pack. Along with the kids from the neighboring apartments, we would walk to school, arrange movie outings on the weekends, or just hang out. We formed soccer teams. I was the only female on the team as a goalie. I was really a tomboy. I preferred to hang out with my brother and his friends than with my sister and her friends. My sister always loved visiting girls her age at their apartments and would sit for hours and chat. I preferred the outside and stayed out until late at night. We were allowed to stay out late only if we stayed within the front or the back of the apartment building.

The building next to us was a private dorm for college girls. I bet my dad had a great time with that. We used to watch them from our balcony. This dorm had a big back yard full of pear trees. They were the most delicious pears I have ever eaten. After dark, we would sneak into their back yard and steal pears.

The kids on Sixth Street became good friends, but this did not happen with the parents. There were too many retired military dads in the building. As you can imagine, their wives were the generals! Each wanted to impose her own rules on how to govern the building. They were like the dogs in a park. They kept marking each other's territories to gain power. For what? Their screams and fights never stopped. It all came to a halt one day when one of the retired military dads pulled a gun at another retired military dad. That day, my dad decided that we should move out. And that was the end of my great carefree six years in Bahçelievler, growing up with a lot of friends.

We ended up moving to the Centrum of Ankara, called Kızılay, which means "Red Crescent", equivalent to the Red Cross in the United States. It took its name from the very old building where the headquarters of the Kızılay was located. It was noisy, we had no friends, and the streets and sidewalks were filled with cars. There was no place to play even if you had a friend. But one great thing about it was that you could walk almost anywhere and hang out. Great cafes and pudding shops were only ten minutes away.

I cried a lot. Days and days. I wonder how my mom felt about it. It must have been very annoying to see your daughter cry for several months. Slowly, I accepted the fact that we could not go back to Bahçelievler. I still miss the years there, filled with childhood memories. I would get purple wrists by playing with a toy—I can't remember what it was called. It consisted of two balls attached to a string that you were supposed to hold in the middle and have the balls collide in the mid-air above and below your wrist. A lot of times, especially while learning, you would miss a lot and the ball would collide with your wrist. I had many nice bumps. The game was so addictive that I ended up wrapping my arms with cloths to prevent more injury to my already purple wrists.

From our Kızılay apartment, I had to take either a bus or *dolmuş* to go to my high school, which was quite far. I avoided buses even though they were cheaper. Unfortunately, during those times girls on buses would get a lot of pinching and pressing. I hated that. Every time it happened, I would yell at the person to embarrass him. But, since it was so annoying to be constantly watching your back, right and left, I chose the *dolmuş*. *Dolmuş* is a seven-passenger large station wagon with three doors, two in the front and one on the back on the passenger side. Every *dolmuş* has a designated route. It picks up anyone, anytime, anywhere and takes the person anywhere on its route. All you have to do is to raise your hand, like you are calling a taxi. And when you are in, all you have to do is to tell the driver where you want to get off.

During my Bahçelievler years and beyond, my best friend was Tuba. She was in the first apartment in Bahçelievler, the one on First Avenue. We were renting the first floor and she was on the third floor. We became friends when we were in third grade. Her father was a congressman from Sivas, a city east of Ankara, and her mom was a French teacher. Her uncle was a senator. They had much higher living standards, and this sometimes showed in our relationship. She was not a great student, so I used to help her a lot. And she helped me a lot to see myself as a young woman rather than a little girl, or a tomboy. My father was okay with me going out with her, and sometimes I would have sleepovers with her. Those were the times I could go out and date without any hint to my dad. She started to date her husband when she was in eighth grade. She married him after finishing college. She was in the same university as I was, and we continued our relationship. However, we were not as close as we were during grade school.

She lives in Portland, Oregon now with her husband and two boys who are older than you are. Once in a while we call each other. She visited us once when her mom and my mom took the same flight to come to the United States to visit their respective daughters. The last time I saw her was in 1999. She was at my wedding reception given by my sister's best friend when we visited Turkey during our honeymoon. The wedding reception was for my family and relatives who could not make it to the United States for our wedding. She sat next to me, and all those years we were apart just disappeared. We sang the songs we used to sing when we were growing up and falling in love with boys. We hugged and we cried. I still miss her. I remember what a "clean freak" she was. She used to wash all her records with soap and water to clean the dirt and finger smudges. I still use her technique when we rent DVDs. She had gorgeous honey-colored hair with beautiful long waves. She had great big green eyes. She once washed her hair with laundry detergent to make it squeaky clean. I remember my sister giving her advice on how bad that was. At that time my sister was in medical school and she was already becoming our house doctor.

I had another very close friend, Neşe, but our friendship ended with high school. She went to dentistry school. Her mother was our mathematics teacher in high school for three years. We, all three of us, used to get together during weekdays and weekends and go out with Tuba's boyfriend's friends. Tuba's boyfriend was in college in Ankara. He used to share an apartment with two other classmates. And they had a great group of friends. I dated a couple of them, but none of them lasted long. I learned a wonderful thing about growing up: hanging out with boys and girls. I listened to Cat Stevens, Carol King, Bob Dylan, The Weavers, The Moody Blues, Pink Floyd, and Jethro Tull. I started to buy my own records to play at my home. We had a small record player that was one of the biggest investments my dad made. My favorite records were by Chopin and Cat Stevens. Whenever I got fed up with studying, I would put on Chopin's *Polonaise* and pretend to be a conductor all around in our living room.

One of the records I had was of Mendelssohn, and included the *Wedding March*. My boyfriend at that time was into music a lot, and he gave me the record as a present. I still wonder if he was trying to hint at something when he gave me that record. He broke up with me within a month. I wonder if he thought I was either oblivious or insensitive. I was just eighteen then.

4

Early School Years

During my time, elementary school used to be five years, followed by three years of middle school and three years of high school. In first grade I was at Yenimahalle İlkokulu. *İlkokul* means "first school." The second year I was at Cebeci İlkokulu. The remaining three years of my elementary school education, I went to Alpaslan İlkokulu in Bahçelievler. Then I went to Deneme Lisesi. Although *lise* means "high school," Deneme Lisesi provided education from sixth grade to eleventh grade. It was a "magnet" high school, and it followed the same teaching structure as the Fen Lisesi, where my dad taught and my brother attended. In my class at Deneme Lisesi there were about twenty-five students, and many of us went on to medical, dentistry, engineering, science, and business administration schools. There might have been only two students in my class who could not get into college. One of them was the class clown, who would bring a two-liter Coke bottle to the class and make his own long straw by combining several straws and make really funny sounds when we were in class. He used to sit right behind me and kept putting pencils in my curls throughout the entire class.

In Alpaslan İlkokulu I had the nicest teacher in the world. She was exactly like my mom. She even looked like my mom, with curly red hair. She was very soft-spoken. I still remember her telling us calmly to quiet down. The class abused her, as any group of little kids would do. Kids can act like darlings when they are alone, but are really mean creatures as a pack, and when they smell weakness, they pounce on it. That is exactly what was happening to my teacher. One day, she could not take it any longer. Teary-eyed, she left the class. Then the vice principal came, a really mean lady who sounded like the principal in *Matilda*, by Roald Dahl. She told us that if we did not behave when our teacher came back, she would rip our legs apart. Boy! That scared us. We begged and cried for hours.

We badly wanted our teacher back. She came back the next day. We all were as quiet as a mouse and were really good to her afterwards. I guess in our minds we realized that our teacher was a gift to us and no other teacher could replace her. We also realized how lucky we were when we encountered the possible replacement for her.

I used to walk to school with my brother. My brother was only a year ahead of me. Since our family was still paying my grandfather's debts, we never had money to buy decent clothes. I would wear my sister's hand-me-downs. At least they were close to my size. However, since we did not have another boy in the family, my parents would buy my brother winter coats about two sizes larger than he was, hoping that he would wear them at least three or four years. Poor thing would disappear in the bulkiness of thick wool coats. I remember his big brown coat with a belt. When he got itchy he would go to a tree and rub his back like a little bear. During those times, until about college age, my brother and I were not very close. I assumed he was not comfortable walking with me to school. That is absolutely not cool! He was embarrassed to be seen with his younger sister. For many years, until he grew like an asparagus in early spring, I was taller than he was. I was his annoying younger sister, following his footsteps just a year behind, until he went to Fen Lisesi. Fen Lisesi was a boarding school. After that, we only saw him some Wednesday evenings for dinner and on the weekends. My mom would cook his favorite meals, and we would wait excitedly for him to ring the bell. He always had a bag of nonperishable food when he returned to school. One of the things my mom always packed for him was a jar of honey mixed with butter for him to eat at night with the bread he could get from his cafeteria.

Now he is six foot two and a very handsome doctor. I guess he does not mind spending hours with me. He begs me to come live in his town. We miss each other a lot and talk on the phone constantly.

I had a neighbor kid, Sermet, who lived upstairs during our first three years in Bahçelievler. He and I were in the same class. Every morning when the school bell rang, we would race to our class to be the first to enter. I still get that adrenaline rush when I am going somewhere. I am never late to any of my meetings or dinner arrangements. As you probably figured out by now, I cannot stand people being late. Anybody who is late for a meeting appears not to care about the people at the meeting, and that is unacceptable for me. I don't even like my own rule on this. And I know you don't either. You probably remember many times arriving at a doctor's office twenty minutes early or waiting for our friends at a restaurant sitting and twirling our thumbs.

I was an excellent student and was assigned many duties at school. I was always selected to read my own poems at school events. I had a notebook with all my poems. I wish I had saved that notebook. During our elementary school graduation, that is at the end of the fifth grade, I was supposed to cite my latest poem. I thought I would know it by heart since I wrote it. I became overconfident. When I got on the stage, I forgot all my lines. I felt horrible. I got really embarrassed. There was no way out, and it felt really bad. It took me months to recover from that heavy feeling you get in your chest when you have done something wrong and you cannot go back and change it. That event was the end of my poetry days. I did not write any more poems until my grandmother died. It was very sad to lose her. It felt like losing a piece of my history, my past, my childhood, all gone.

I was visiting her and my Kara Dede the first time I went back to Turkey after three years in the United States. It was my first winter break as an assistant professor at Alfred University. First I spent time with my parents and siblings, and then I took a bus to Taşucu, just like the old times. After a couple of days with my grandparents, I said goodbye to them. I knew I was saying goodbye to her for the last time. She had a broken arm in a cast. Her Alzheimer's was at such a level that she knew no one. She thought I was my grandfather's lover, and yelled at me. She had hallucinations. Actually, this all started when the government took over our olive grove to build a paper factory on it. They cut down almost all the trees except a few left for landscaping. These trees had been planted one by one by my grandmother. They were just seedlings. For many years, she tended them and watched them grow. She used to talk to them and touch them as if they were her children. They were beautiful trees with shimmering leaves, green on one side and silver on the other. It hurt her deeply, as if she had lost her soul, her babies. She cried for a long time. She was also suffering from migraines. My grandfather gave her medicine every night, before he sneaked out to see the "lady of easy virtue." He gave her a brain-frying drug that was later banned but was sold over the counter as pain medication at that time. It was Optalidon, which basically consisted of butabarbital, aminophenazone, and caffeine. I don't know what effect it had on her. She eventually developed Alzheimer's. She stopped doing all the house chores. My grandfather took over the cooking. He eventually removed the gas stove from the house because, when he was away, she would turn the burners on and forget to light them in an attempt to cook something. Neighbors helped, bringing food daily, and Kara Dede supplemented that with restaurant food. She got worse quickly. She did not even notice that her arm was broken until my sister found out while doing regular checkups with her. They put her arm in a cast, and she died that way. When I saw her wandering on the streets of Taşucu, I knew that it was the last time I would be seeing her. When the taxi started to pull out, after I hugged both of my grandparents dearly, I looked back and saw her waddling side to side with a broken arm, wrinkly face, same type of dress that my mother had sewn for her in the last thirty some years. She was just a fragile little body taking one of her daily walks from which she would not know how to return. I cried and wanted to go back and hug her once more, but I knew it meant nothing. I knew it was time to say goodbye to her and move on. I quietly said my farewell, and I knew then I would miss her but cherish her memories the rest of my life and pass them on to you. I cried more that day than the day my dad called me to say that she had passed away. She had died in her sleep at her home of fifty plus years. You never had a chance to meet her. She died three years before you were born. She had a great influence on us as a hard-working and strong woman. She was a good grandmother and had unconditional love for her grandkids, but she never spoiled us in the ways my grandfather did. She said what she believed and never compromised or bent.

She was one of those people called "aged soil," as in Turkish *eski toprak,* one who had more things to give and say than to take.

The day I heard that she was no longer with us; I sat down and wrote my first poem after almost fifteen years. It was about her and her olive trees and life in Taşucu. I bought a small poster of one of Van Gogh's olive grove paintings, can't remember which one, I guess it was *Olive Grove with Picking Figures*. When I went to Turkey that summer, I went to her grave and buried the poster and the poem next to her. I hope it became part of the soil that she became. I did not make a copy of the poem, it was only for her. I did not write any poems after that until I had marriage troubles with your dad.

Back to My School Years

A typical cycle for me during middle school and high school was to study hard, get A's, and cry if I didn't get A's. Come home from school or from outings with friends. Hope that my dad would not be home for a while so I could enjoy the peace with my mom and my siblings. Forget anything that happened that day upon seeing mom's face. Get a hug from her at the entrance of our apartment. Kiss those soft cheeks and hug her as if she would break. Visit my grandparents during winter and summer breaks. Those were wonderful, delicious years. I can still smell the tea, cookies, my mom's hair, my grandfather's hat, and remember the wonderful times we had around our dinner table.

During my adolescence I read a lot of books, mostly by Turkish and Russian authors. I got depressed with Dostoyevski and warmed to my country with Yasar Kemal and Nazım Hikmet. I learned a lot, imagined a lot, and studied a lot. Everything was fascinating. All those times I felt like there was a core that I was sitting in that protected me. My core was my mom, my grandparents, my sister and brother, and to some degree my father. I was feeling very secure with this core. And I could reach out and try things and go back to the core to refuel myself if I got hurt. This core was my house. It was my house that contained more of me than I showed you in my *avlu*.

I had a lot of time to read since I often was not allowed to go out with my friends. Well, it was kind of good that I could just cozy up on our couch and read for hours and share the sun-filled room with my mother. But I was always angry at my dad for not allowing us the "normal" life that my friends had. He never let my sister and me do anything outside of our house, not even go to the movies with our friends after we reached adolescence. My girlfriends' parents were much more relaxed about going out with friends. So I fibbed a lot. I don't think I ever told him the right information when I went out with my friends. I will not call these lies, because for me and for my mother, who knew the real truth about my whereabouts, these were harmless fibs that only protected me and never hurt anybody. I assume that it even helped my dad to think that he had the most obedient girls on earth. We were great students with no troubles. This is really any parent's dream. Of course my mother had to go through the entire parenting process all by herself. She listened to our outpourings about boyfriends, school, friends, troubles, and complaints about our dad.

We even spent many hours a week trying to convince her that she should stand up for her rights. But she never told anyone about her rights and desires, she never complained about anyone to anybody. She accepted her role and tried to make the best of it. That was who she was.

I never fully became my mother or my father. I was not like my dad. I never brushed you away with "just because I am your mother and I told you so." I was not like my mom. Because I did not want to be abused by being too soft. I am not so sure which was the right thing to do. I tried very hard not to be my dad or my mom. Those would have been easy roles for me to fall into. Especially, being my dad. I had every gene he had. I have a quick temper. I had to fight with myself not to yell at you, and I know I did sometimes. But you and I were never shy about talking for many hours. I also told you that I would not be angry if you had done something wrong as long as you told the truth. Everybody makes mistakes. I made my share of mistakes, sometimes pretty big ones, without thinking of the consequences. I told you that those things are part of your growth and I wanted to share with you, to guide you, not to punish you. You are here to have a life to enjoy, to learn from, to create, and to pass on. I am so honored to be part of that. And I would do anything for you to make your life better and more meaningful. You know that I am here for you.

5

College Years

My dream in high school was to get into and graduate from the Middle East Technical University in Ankara, get a Ph.D. in the United States and then come back as a professor to the same university, and stay in those beautiful two-story faculty housing units. It was highly prestigious to teach at that university. It was the best technical university in the country and maybe in the Middle East region. It had a huge campus just outside of Ankara, covered with trees planted by the first groups of students when the university was founded in 1956, the year before I was born. When I pass by the campus now, I cannot even see the buildings through the trees. The entire campus is literally in a forest. It has its own cherry orchard and a lake. There are large buildings sprawled around on acres and acres of land.

Since education in the university is all in English, the entering freshmen were required to have certain knowledge of English. Like everyone else, I took the English qualification test, but failed miserably. I had to attend the "prep school," year "zero" on campus, a one-year "English-only" program. That was a very light and fun year. I was in the university environment and taking one course, English, which lasted all day long. The classes were held in a small building, farthest away from the center of campus activities and major buildings. That year I did a lot of walking and met a lot of new friends. After prep school, when I started freshman year, my grades dropped like a rock. I was coming from one of the best high schools and I had my dad's genes. I was so sure about my knowledge and about my intelligence that I paid little attention to the classes. My grade point average (GPA) for the first two years was around 2.5. It was a good wake-up call for me to realize that over-confidence really does play bad tricks on you. Since I had a goal to get my Ph.D., a 2.5 GPA would never take me there. Finally, during my third and the fourth years in college I worked really hard and moved my GPA to over 3.5. I was determined to finish my master's at the Middle East Technical University and go to the United States for a Ph.D. There was no time to fool around.

Of course, college was not easy. I was in engineering and the courses were really difficult. On top of that, there were a lot of political activities going on at the campus. Those were the years of left and right movements going on full scale. The protests against the government and the government's reaction to protests were not that peaceful. Water spraying, tear gassing, and shootings were the norm. One of my classmates was killed during one of the events. There was a consensus outside the Middle East Technical University that the entire university was under the control of the leftists. The story was that the faculty and students were extremely liberal and they were fighting for their rights. Slowly, we saw a change in the non-teaching personnel. Right-wing people started to work at cafeterias, buildings, university grounds, and dormitories. One day when the students were protesting against this purposeful move, somebody threw a bomb in the middle of the student body. There was a loud explosion, dust, and chaos. There were some injuries. I cannot remember if there were any casualties that day, but I remember running. Thousands of us were running. One of my friends was asking me if I had any extra shoes (!) with me since she lost one of hers in the commotion. We all ran to the dormitories, which were at least a good twenty-minute walk from the main buildings. Then we had a lockdown and demanded that the government send military troops to protect us. Half the people locked down at the dorms were not residents at the dormitories. Like me, many students commuted every day. We used to take the university buses, all blue with the university logo on them, from and to Ankara. That day we demanded that the military pull our buses in front of the dorms and form a corridor lined up with soldiers so that students could walk to the buses without getting shot. The bombing happened early in the afternoon. It was midnight by the time the buses came. In the middle of the night, about fifty blue buses carried hungry and tired students to the city. When I reached home, it was already past midnight. My parents, my brother, my sister, and Güngör Abi were waiting. They said they glued themselves to the television all day, watching the events unfold. They still say that was one of the scariest days of their lives. The news had been reporting injuries, and they were not releasing any names. For almost twelve hours nobody could call home to say "I am not hurt." How horrible it must be to see your children go to college and have to worry about them being killed.

6

I Married Your Dad

I had a wide range of friends, and dated here and there. I met your dad during my sophomore year when he transferred from the electrical engineering department to my department, industrial engineering. He definitely showed every sign of being a very serious and smart man. That was the attraction point for me, and it would become one of the reasons for divorce many years later. We went out in our senior year. We were both accepted to our department's master's program in operations research, and it looked like a perfect match.

Your dad became a teaching assistant while studying for his master's degree, and I had to find work. I finally got into the National Productivity Institute, a government research organization. The place was very supportive of my attendance to complete my master's degree. Your dad and I got married in October of that year, 1980. A year later, on September 9, 1981, I came to the United States. Your dad's arrival was three weeks prior to mine. The summer of 2005 was the year that split my time on earth equally in two countries, twenty-four years in each country.

Your dad and I started dating in June 1979. We used to share an office as teaching assistants to our professors for junior classes. We spent most of our time in the office when we did not have classes. It was a privilege to have an assistant desk at that time. After dating a few months, we got engaged.

Our generation was probably the first generation in which dating became an acceptable social event in the cities, but not to my father. Most of the time people followed the path to a traditional arranged marriage, which involved quite a number of rituals, as my parents had done. So for the new generation, to make the parents happy, couples who decided to get married created a "faux" arranged marriage process. The boy's parents would visit the girl's parents' house to ask the girl's father for her hand in marriage. And the famous talk would happen, "Our kids love each other and they want to marry. We would like them to be happy. We are asking your permission to have my son marry your daughter." After the official "yes," the wine and beer would follow with fruits and pastry to celebrate the event. That is when the boy and the girl are referred to as *sözlü* (meaning "promised"), not yet *nişanlı* (meaning "engaged"). And the boy and the girl would wear *sözlü* rings—a very thin gold or silver band on their left index fingers. The engagement ring comes with the engagement party. Thicker, traditional, wedding bands are placed on the right index fingers during the ceremony at the engagement party. It is very rare for a middle income family to buy a diamond ring for the girl, so the only way you knew the person was engaged was to look at the right index finger, where the band was. The ring would then be transferred to the left index finger at the wedding ceremony.

Our wedding was very simple. In Turkey, the girl's side pays for the engagement and the boy's side pays for the wedding. Since both parents were typical middle income families, we both opted for the cheapest solution. In Ankara, if you are not planning a wedding reception at a ballroom or a restaurant, you can get married at a municipal building just reserved for weddings. You get a ten-minute slot in the wedding hall, which allows your guests to walk in, sit down, and watch you get married on a platform with two witnesses and an official from the Ankara municipality, and then leave the seating area at once. It all happens in ten minutes. Then the next couple and the guests would push in to get the best of their ten-minute slot. I wonder what would happen if a bride or a groom had an urgent need to go to the bathroom! The official from the municipality should write a book about unusual wedding moments. After the ceremony, the newlywed couple and their families line up in a corner and greet their guests. A youngster from the family gives the wedding treats, usually candies wrapped in tulle.

I made my wedding treats on the day Turkey had another military coup. We woke up one September morning with a call from my friend telling us to turn the radio on. We rushed towards the windows. Since we were living in the Centrum of Ankara, we could see the tanks rolling down the streets, blocking major roadways. The radio was blasting military marching music and announcing an all-day curfew. Then I remembered that the day before, while on the bus to my university, there were military convoys, miles long, moving towards Ankara. I thought it was just a practice operation. While listening to the radio and TV all day, I put three candied almonds and one chocolate truffle into a tulle piece and tied them with raffia. And I repeated this 120 times. I sat by our big window overlooking the main street in Ankara and watched the tanks roll into the Centrum.

A few days before the wedding date, your dad won a very prestigious scholarship from the Turkish Scientific Research Institute (Türkiye Bilimsel Teknik Araştırma Merkezi, *TÜBİTAK*). That was his ticket to the United States for his Ph.D. And it was also my ticket to go with him to do my Ph.D., but without a scholarship.

I actually had a scholarship from the same institute during high school and the first two years in college. There was a very tough written exam followed by an oral exam. The oral exam was given by panels of mathematics and physics professors. I made it. I was already doing great at the national physics, mathematics, and chemistry competitions. The scholarship of 150 liras a month was great money in my time. It covered my daily allowance and clothes without having to ask for money from my father. My brother had the same scholarship, and that was a big relief for my dad. During those times, it was uncommon for kids from middle income families to work. First of all, there weren't many jobs for youths. For us, the job was to do well at school. Within the first few months of receiving my scholarship, my dad asked me if I would pay for the household electricity. I refused. That was my money. I would have agreed to it if we were really in trouble. He was gambling, and I did not want my own sweat money to go to his gambling.

Your dad had a different path though. Although his father was a doctor, he retired early and did not support your dad very much. So your dad worked throughout his college years. I remember him coming to my parents' house from the Centrum, freezing from selling New Year's cards out on the street.

Our first apartment was a basement flat, a thirty-minute *dolmuş* ride from my parents. It was a filthy, cockroach-infested, moldy, smelly place. The rent was equivalent to my salary—that of a freshly graduated industrial engineer from the top technical school in Turkey. You could create the same story here: take an engineer the first year out of school, tell him that he has to live in New York City and ask him to rent a place. That is exactly what he would end up doing. Either he will share the rental place, or if he is married, one salary would go to the landlord. I was literally getting my salary from the bank, carrying it to my landlord's apartment across the street, and handing him my whole salary—not a penny was left over. We lived on what your dad was making, a bit more than my salary. We spent a year in that house and finished our master's degrees. Your Uncle Aykut, your dad's youngest brother, was also living with us. He was a medical student then. We were feeding three mouths with some help from my parents. I remember one day coming home and seeing that our dinner for that night, which we had prepared the night before, was all gone. Aykut was just hungry coming from school and ate it all without leaving anything for us.

All of our furniture was borrowed or hand-me-downs. Since we knew we were coming to the United States, my parents bought the new furniture that they were planning to buy for us for themselves and gave us their old furniture. We bought used kitchen supplies from our relatives. I think the only new things in our house were the mattress and the linens. We did not have a bed frame or a box-spring. Our mattress was on the cold floor. And it was another pretty harsh winter, where you could feel cold seeping through the mattress into your bones.

Your dad and I did not have much time alone in our apartment. First, your dad's parents stayed with us for more than a month right after our wedding. Given that we did not go for a honeymoon, we literally started to live with your dad's parents. After they left, the furnace in my family's apartment building stopped working due to the coal shortage, and my entire family moved in with us: Kara Dede, Büyükanne, my mom, my dad, my two year old nephew Tolga, my sister, my brother-in-law, and sometimes my brother. We had no washer. We had to take all our laundry to my parents' apartment to wash. Can you imagine, for two months, every week, we carried the laundry of about ten people to my parents' apartment. Of course, there was no heat there. Everything was frozen. We sat there in our coats, hats, and gloves to get the laundry done. And we had to carry all that wet, heavy wash back to our apartment to dry. There were no dryers in Turkey at that time. My parents still don't own one. We would spread the laundry all around the rooms. Nice humidifier! There were no laundromats in Turkey at that time either. Our evenings at my house actually were very cozy. Unfortunately, my grandmother's Alzheimer's was at a high level. She would constantly complain about Kara Dede bringing whores into her house. Those whores were us, her grandchildren. We could never convince her that we were her family.

After our one-year stay in that bug hole, we sold all our furniture to my aunt's husband. That money became my first-semester tuition, and we were ready to go to Buffalo.

7

Off to Buffalo

Why did we choose Buffalo? Very simple. We already had a friend there who had started his Ph.D. one year before us, and we did not know anything about Buffalo's winters. It was gray and dark, with empty streets, rusty cars, freezing rain, and mounds of snow. It was very depressing. I was there from September 1981 until April 1984. Unfortunately, I continued to stay in upstate New York for another four years.

Think about your mom, who spent many of her months in the Mediterranean region. For her, Ankara was a very cold city, a high plateau with no warm breezes from the sea, with dry and hot summers, and with snow in the winter. But nothing matched Buffalo's lake-effect snow.

Your dad left Turkey almost a month before I did. My papers did not come on time. I was going with an F2 visa, as the wife of a student. I was already accepted to SUNY Buffalo's industrial engineering department. I still do not remember why I ended up applying for an F2 visa. After I became a student, I converted it to an F1 visa. For about three weeks after your dad left I chased the postman up and down the street. My papers were lost twice, time was flying by, and it was getting late to start the fall semester. Finally, one morning, my visa papers showed up in the mail. I took a taxi to the American Embassy, got my visa, and went to a travel agency to get my ticket. My dad borrowed money for me for the Ankara to New York flight. I borrowed money from Güngör Abi for the New York to Buffalo flight. I went home and finished packing. The next morning, with my entire family saying goodbye at the airport, I left Ankara for an unknown future. I did not return for a visit for three years, three months, and three days. I had only 1500 dollars savings in my pocket from selling our household goods to my aunt. These 1500 dollars was my ticket to a new life, and I was ready to work hard not to fail and not to come back with my wings down. This was almost like gambling: this money was enough for the first semester only. If I got an assistantship, I could continue to complete my Ph.D. If not, I had to ask my parents to send me a ticket to go back home. I did not even have enough money to buy a return ticket. Neither did my parents.

Here is what I packed in my luggage: a couple of sweaters, my famous black merino turtleneck that I still wear, enough underwear to last for a week, socks, a winter coat, hat, gloves, one pair of shoes, pajamas, T-shirts, shirts, a couple of pairs of pants, and a couple of skirts. I could not fit any more clothes in one suitcase, and my parents did not have money to buy me another one. I left my grandfather's blanket behind. Three years later, that was the first thing I brought back with me. I paid my dad and brother-in-law back on my first return trip to Ankara. I did not want to owe any money, even to my dad. I could easily give money to my parents, my sister, and my brother. But it was hard for me to owe money to anyone, including my parents. As of today, the only debt I have is our home mortgage.

The minute I purchased my tickets to the United States, I called the only telephone number I had to reach your dad. It was the number of a few Turkish students living together. Your dad stayed with them for a few days. He had already moved into an apartment in which four Turkish people—your dad and I and two other Turkish friends—would be sharing for the next several months. The new place did not have a telephone yet. I left a message on the Turkish kids' answering machine. I was hoping by the time they got the message they would have more than twenty-four hours to let your dad know that I was coming and he would meet me at the airport. This was again one of my "rush things." I waited so long for my papers to come, and the minute they came, I acted as if I was too late. Too late for what? By that time I had already missed my registration deadline, and I had already decided I would wait for the next semester. Instead, I just bought my ticket for the next day and left immediately. I should have stayed at least a few days extra to spend a relaxed time with my family. I left them in shock. All of sudden, in one day, their little daughter was just gone like a puff in the air. And none of us knew that we would not be seeing each other for three years.

The rest of my last day in Turkey, I completed my packing. The hours flew by. My parents, my sister, my brother-in-law, my dear nephew Tolga, and my brother all gathered at my parents' house, almost like having the last supper. I never realized at that time how hard this was for my family, especially my mother. I can now imagine sending you to a faraway place that would take at least twelve hours to fly to, and not knowing when I would see you again. My dear mother, she kept her tears to herself. My grandfather and grandmother were also with us for a month. Later I realized that this was arranged by my grandfather so that he could say goodbye to me. I learned later that they left Ankara just a few days after I left. Oh, how I miss them. The morning of my flight all of us piled into two cars, with my one suitcase in the trunk, and drove to the airport. I remember the moment I started to walk towards the passport control. Tolga, who was then three and a half years old, was the only one who started to cry and begged me not to go. His arms were reaching behind the bars separating us. My entire family was quietly saying goodbye to me. My heart was pounding—I was facing the unknown and leaving my dear family behind. I was scared, sad, petrified, but also excited going to my new life. I don't think I would do a similar thing now. These things happen when you are young. You are ready then to conquer the world. Taste the unknown. Take risks. Because you feel that you are invincible and brave. Just like in one of my favorite songs by Cat Stevens, "Father and Son." Father asks his son to settle down and get married, and the son wants change and wants to move out. Now I know both sides, and I know how hard it was for my family.

I left for the gate. I switched gears in my head and started to look forward, not back anymore. I boarded the PanAm airplane, destination Frankfurt. From there I would switch to a plane to New York. I had the least enjoyable flight of my life. I had a hard time understanding the flight attendants. When they served me my meal, I could not figure out what the little plastic container had in it. I ate my salad with no olive oil and no lemon juice, thinking that the Americans do not use anything on their salad! I watched the entire Superman movie without ear phones since they were charging four dollars for them. Four dollars was a lot of money for me. I was flying to the unknown and all I had was 1500 dollars, and most of it was for my college tuition. The minute I left Turkey I realized how bad my conversational English was. In the Middle East Technical University, we had all our classes in English—all technical, of course—but most of our professors were Turkish. They would lecture in English, but we could ask our questions in Turkish. I could write term papers in English and take exams in English, but I could not converse in English. I did not have a vocabulary for daily English.

I arrived in New York at JFK airport on the afternoon of September 9, 1981. My father arranged for someone to meet me at the gate. My dad's friend, who happened to be the gambling-club owner, asked her brother, a ground manager for PanAm at JFK to meet me. He sent one of his employees, an American, whom I hardly understood, to help me find my flight to Buffalo. This gentleman greeted me after the customs and helped me get my luggage transferred to my destination flight. He put me on the terminal bus to take me to the TWA terminal. It took him five rounds of explanations for me to understand about my next flight. When he was saying "TWA," all I was hearing was "two double a" and I was wondering what it was about. Finally he showed it to me on my ticket, letter by letter. I waited five hours for my "two double a" flight. It was getting dark. I was all alone at the terminal, and was literally all alone in the world. I was hungry. I munched on the bread I had saved from my last flight. My only hope was that in a few hours I would see your dad at the airport when I landed in Buffalo.

I knew that it was a short flight to Buffalo. The plane landed after about forty minutes. There was an announcement that I could not understand. I picked up my belongings and left the plane, wondering why everyone was so slow to leave. Most passengers were still sitting around. I was proud of myself for being so quick that I would be one of the first ones out of the plane. Yes, I was indeed. I started to walk through the airport and started seeing signs saying "Welcome to Syracuse." It did not dawn on me until after the ninth sign. And I ran back to the plane as fast as I could. I was mortified. What would I do if the plane left without me, which could have been the last plane out of Syracuse to Buffalo that day? All my clothes were in my one and only suitcase, and I knew no one in Syracuse. I made it to the plane. I felt like an idiot, feeling the smiles of fellow passengers. I could imagine what they were thinking.

The flight arrived at Buffalo around eight at night. There was no one at the airport to meet me. I waited and waited, sitting on my suitcase and hoping someone would show up. All I knew was the street address of where your dad and two other Turkish friends lived. I gave up around nine-thirty or so. The airport was getting quiet, and I started to worry that staying there would not be that safe. I got into a taxi and handed the driver the address. He did not recognize the street name, and the address was wrongly written as Buffalo instead of Allenhurst, which is a section of Buffalo. After studying his map for twenty minutes, he finally located the street. After about a thirty-minute ride from the airport, we came to a wide street lined with trees and single homes. The street sign brought me big relief. All during that thirty-minute ride I was thinking of all kinds of bad things happening to me and no one finding out anything about it.

Then I saw three figures walking down the street—your dad and the two friends we were to share the house with. I stopped the taxi and jumped out. They were shocked. They had no idea I was coming; no one had reached them with the information. We all piled into the taxi, and a few minutes later, I stepped out of the taxi in front of the first place I called home in the United States: a garden apartment with two bedrooms upstairs and a living room and a kitchen downstairs. Typical student housing. Run down, dirty, but still a home. The hardwood floor was covered with grime, the walls were dirty, the kitchen cabinets probably were never washed, and there were only a few pieces of furniture. This was worse than what we had in Ankara. At least there were no cockroaches.

An hour later, two undergraduates showed up, both Turks, coming to inform your dad that I was arriving that day.

That night I tasted, in horror, typical American bread and my first peanut butter and jelly sandwich. I loved the peanut butter and jelly, but I was heartbroken about the bread. It was just an edible sponge—no crust, no bread taste. I realized that my challenge was not just school. It was also adjusting to a different culinary taste. The heaviness in my heart kept growing. I had a restless night. I missed my family with their images imprinted in my mind when they were waving goodbye at the airport. I still cry thinking about those moments, especially Tolga's cry. He was the one I missed the most for three years before I went back for my visit the first time.

My First Day in the United States

After spending hours together with your dad, our roommates—also from Turkey and attending the same university—and our newly acquired friends, who failed to let your dad know about my coming, we went to bed. That was my first night in the United States: in a small room with a borrowed mattress and a box spring, a cardboard box as a night stand, old sheets for curtains, and a small table as a study desk. I had this strange feeling when I woke up. A completely strange house, a completely strange country. A complete change of life to pursue my dreams—a funny dream, that is. To get a Ph.D. so that I could teach at my university so that I can stay at those lovely homes that are provided for the faculty! Well, I said to myself, I am here now and must make the best of it. Like any other survival story, I did not want to be placed in that certain percentage of those who quit. One of your dad's friends did just that. He missed his mom's *köfte* and stayed only one semester and then moved back to Turkey. At least, when I left Turkey, I took my black agenda book with all my mom's recipes for my favorite foods. I still have it. The year on the agenda book was 1973. In addition to recipes, it still has my notes while I was studying for the national chemistry competition in my senior year in high school.

But I did not want to rush to start school. I was late. The university was already in session and my TOEFL (Test of English as a Foreign Language) score was not high enough for the future possibility of getting an assistantship. I just did not want to risk not being able to study for TOEFL while taking classes. I thought I would get used to my new life, learn my way around, and study English. And I thought the weather would be better during the spring semester. Boy, was I wrong!

When we woke up the next morning, I went to the university's campus with your dad. We could walk from home to the main campus in about twenty minutes, and then take the shuttle to the Amherst campus where the school of engineering was. I met with the professor who was heading the human factors engineering program in the industrial engineering department, Dr. Colin Drury. He was from Great Britain, and definitely had the look of a professor—gray hair, gray beard, tall, and very energetic with a great Scottish accent.

He received my transcript and gave me the great news that all the courses that I had taken during my master's program in operations research in Turkey counted towards my Ph.D. After I left his office I went to the commons area, curled up on a lounge sofa, and fell asleep. Your dad woke me up. For minutes, I could not comprehend where I was. I was already missing my family. Everything was different. On top of that, I was feeling the big load of responsibilities ahead of me.

The next two-and-a-half years were the toughest years I ever had, feeling the "worry-lump" in my throat, and walking the entire path to graduation full of hunger, anxiety, home-sickness, and loneliness.

But, this is exactly what made me strong enough to face my future. There is a lot out there that we face. If you are not ready, it can literally gobble you up. If you have one of your life puzzle pieces broken or damaged or face a pothole on your path, it is best to have other pieces of your life working well. You need to have a strong inner glue to hold onto so that your life puzzle will not fall apart.

During the first few years away from my family, my inner strength was still coming from the letters I received from my parents, my siblings, and my grandfather. They were there for me. They were feeling what I was going through. Years later, when I was going through a divorce from your father, I had job security and a very understanding manager. When I went through job-related stress, I had a very supportive family: Al and you. I believe I would not be me now if I had not gone through those years in Buffalo. Of course I would not be me if I did not live my life and learn from my mistakes. Mistakes hurt, and sometimes stay in your heart and throat and squeeze you as if there is no air left. But they gradually find their place in your mind and stop hurting all together or stay as a sore spot for years to come. I can never say that I am glad those things happened. Maybe I should. I don't know where I would be if the events of my life had not happened the way they did. I am grateful that I came out stronger every time. I went through difficult and good times in my life, and each left something with me.

But there are things I know very well. Living a very poor lifestyle made me grateful for every dollar I earned. I know that money does not come easily, unless you have a great inheritance, of course. I learned to buy only what is needed and added a bit on top for comfort and joy, but never went shopping just to shop.

I lived those two-and-a-half years with only a little help from my family, which I paid back with my first salary. Although I knew that my sister had money, it never occurred to me that she could help me. I was in the United States with a purpose: to finish my Ph.D., and I was doing it on my own. I decided not to sign up for the fall semester, but still did not want to waste time. I bought a TOEFL study book to raise my TOEFL score higher so that I could get an assistantship. I also placed ads on the university's bulletin boards for one-dollar-a-page typewriting. I had only two customers in three months, which did not help at all. My first customer was a professor who brought over a hundred envelopes that I needed to type the addresses on. No problem. Right! The poor professor came to pick up his envelopes. He had a shock on his face after hearing that I charged him fifty cents an address. He handed me a sixty dollar check. Later I called and told him that that I really overcharged him and gave half of his money back. And I had no clue about the address formats in the United States. Especially the two-letter state codes. Instead of typing the code, I ended up spelling out each state and was proud of myself that I was giving my customer extra value for his money. Think about customer satisfaction! I even used a dictionary to look up the spellings of Massachusetts and Pennsylvania.

My encounters with United States culture started with the differences in basic address formatting. I used stories of my own personal cultural experiences at many tutorials I gave on cross-cultural design. My favorite example of cultural differences is on communication—not with humans but with a dog.

In the first few days I was in Buffalo, one morning, after everyone had gone to school, I decided to go to the nearest grocery store. In Buffalo, nobody walks, except penniless people like me. Everyone drives these salt-eaten (big chunks of body missing), ugly, shapeless devices that you can hardly call cars. They look like wounded old people bitten by sharks. People in Buffalo literally drove everywhere, even a few blocks to the grocery store. Later, I realized this was not an isolated phenomenon that only happened in Buffalo.

So here I am walking alone, and I saw this big German shepherd running towards me, barking and running. I was petrified. You know how I used to be scared of dogs, even the little ones, until our Tornado came to our lives. I screamed with my fully adrenaline-rushed voice, using a typical Turkish call to tell the dog to go away: "*Hoşt!*" It does not mean anything really. The German shepherd froze when he heard the word, his head tilted as if he was surprised but curious at the same time, trying to figure out what I was saying. He looked like he was bewildered. I was not going to wait to see the rest of his reaction. I did not care. I used that precious moment to step back to the corner and ran back home. I did not go outside alone for days. Afterwards, I always carried a stick with me, ready to strike anything that could be a potential danger.

Season Changes in Buffalo

The fall of 1981 was the first year that I saw full-scale fall foliage. Everywhere the leaves were turning into spectacular color palettes. Ankara has its four seasons, but you do not see fall foliage like you do in Buffalo.

Maybe there were not enough trees in Ankara and maybe the trees were not the kind whose leaves turn into all shades of red, yellow, and brown. In Ankara, as I remember, the leaves used to turn into just brown. As a first-time foliage watcher, I ended up having my picture taken under almost every beautiful tree that I found.

After overcoming my fear of that German shepherd, I started to walk everywhere. That is the time I fell in love with maps. I found back roads to shops, parks, and open fields. I enjoyed every bit of the season. I put my face into the leaves and opened my eyes to see nothing else but just the colors of the leaves. I loved the sun rays going through the leaves, intensifying their already brilliant colors. The leaves felt soft, refreshing, and soothing. But, somehow they were giving me a feeling of melancholy. I always thought about my mom. I thought how she would have loved the fall colors in Buffalo. Years later, I brought her to see just that, not in Buffalo, but in New Jersey.

But the fall was very short-lived. It got pretty cold by the end of October. We moved to a new apartment the beginning of November. It was just your dad and I. Our friends moved to the lower level of a house a block from our new apartment. We had only one bedroom, a small living room, a pretty large kitchen, and a bathroom. We found some furniture at garage sales and on the curbs left by people as garbage. We bought a used mattress for twenty dollars, sheets for one dollar, a set of six dishes for one dollar, and a television for twenty dollars. We were like birds making a nest for winter. We had only the basics. We did not even have a comforter, just two blankets. That was a mistake. I did not anticipate the cold and snow in Buffalo. It snowed like blankets. They rarely closed the schools, except during long blizzards when the entire city shut down for a week. I thought Ankara had a lot of snow. I remember in winters, my sister, Güngör Abi, my brother, and I would go to the center of the city, only four blocks away from where we lived. We used to have snowball fights right in the middle of the roundabout where the two major boulevards intersected. I loved the silence the snow brought to the city. The busiest section of the city would turn into a ghost town. With that silence, one becomes just oneself. Nothing else matters. You feel elated.

Well that soft, beautiful snow concept completely changed with my Buffalo experience. When the first blizzard hit, I saw how the amount of snow there would impact our lives. We had snow piled up inside, between the window and the plastic insulation we put on the windows to reduce the draft. We always wore our coats, hats, and gloves in the house. It was great going to school since there was heat there. Sometimes, I took my clothes to the gym to take showers there. Instead of pajamas, I wore three sweaters, double socks, and a hat when I went to bed.

Your dad pushed a pin through the thermostat to stop the automatic turn-on when the temperature went below fifty degrees. There were days that our house temperature was below forty degrees. We did not have any money for heating. I had only 150 dollars to spend on rent and food—equally divided. Forget about buying clothes, even a pair of socks. With that limited amount of money, you can understand how creative you can get in spending. Every morning when I got up, I would rush to the kitchen to put the kettle on the stove. There would be a thick covering of ice inside all of our windows. I had to scrape the ice to see what the weather was like that day. We could not afford to take a shower every day. We never did sweat anyway. I would do a quick cleaning in the kitchen, while the boiling water for tea would lower the cold inside the kitchen a few degrees. I would dress up next to the boiling pot. Since I had only a few changes of clothing, it was very easy to figure out what to wear every day. Just wear what is clean. Our refrigerator ended up totally rusted from the cold and the steam in the kitchen.

While busying myself spending the fall semester at home studying TOEFL and doing just two typing jobs, my first Thanksgiving and Christmas came. I took the TOEFL and raised my score to a level that would not interfere anymore with my potential assistantship.

I spent the fall finding the cheapest food stores, and bought only the foods that were on sale. We had two small, bright orange, very thin, nylon backpacks that were given to us when we opened our M&T Bank accounts. I used that backpack everywhere—from lugging food from the grocery store to carrying laundry. With the backpack full of five pounds of potatoes, bread, detergent, vegetables, rice, and ground beef, I felt like the soldiers carrying a stone-filled backpack for their exercises. We ate two pounds of ground beef a month. That was our meat ration. I would divvy up the meat into five little balls and freeze them. This would last us four or five weeks. One becomes very creative in cooking when there is a limited amount of supplies. I would make soup with a tablespoon of tomato paste, flour, salt and water. Talk about the frugal gourmet!

The first year, the cold and lack of nutrition took a toll on our bodies. I remember your dad getting very sick during the winter holidays. I had to walk four miles in the blizzard (and this is not a joke, like your parents bragging about how hard they lived) to a friend's house to get medicine for him. We had no vitamin supplements. I am still paying for those years of malnutrition—from cavities in my teeth, to hypothyroidism to having surgeries every couple of years. My immune system was totally messed up at that time.

After having our surprised shock on Thanksgiving—no place was open and we ended up eating just bread and soup—we were ready for Christmas. The day before Christmas, I walked to the nearest supermarket, which was about a mile away, and bought a case of Labbatts beer and carried the case home. It was a stupid thing to do. Sometimes I wonder why I did all those things. I learned later that it really does not help to go an extra mile in getting things done. People do not applaud all the wonderful things you take care of. They get used to it and lean on you to do everything. It becomes a thankless job. I used to bring up as a conversation topic what I did just to get a bit of appreciation. Well, I am my Kara Dede's granddaughter. I carry some of him with me. I am an *aferin delisi* (remember? "crazy for just praise"). I am a sucker for appreciation.

Your dad was good at helping me with my courses. He was always the pusher in the family. A real hard worker. That is why he finished all his Ph.D. work and dissertation in eighteen months. I was not too bad; I did it in twenty-five months. It took many long sleepless days, nights, and weeks. I think living in Buffalo helped. There was nothing else to do, especially if you did not have money. I bet it would have taken me several years if I studied in New York or in California. I would probably be going out a lot, partying, just like you said you would like to do when you go to college. You never know.

Your dad used to call me "the party girl" because I liked hanging out with people, singing and dancing. Nothing beats that. It is true that I like parties and friends, but I am definitely not a party girl. One thing I always made sure of: I did not jeopardize my studies, my work, or my motherhood for partying and hanging out with friends. I hope you will find a balance in your life between work and social life, and won't get lost in either one of them.

Your priority is to feel good about yourself. And nothing makes you feel better than success, even success in your marriage. Success is intoxicating, you become addicted, and you continue to strive for more. Sometimes you fall down, events happen, you fail. But if you keep your mind open and reach for higher grounds, you will always get up—you get your gears strengthened from the mistakes you learned—and continue on your path. This does not happen by itself. You are the one who can make this happen. Just believe in yourself and enjoy life full of your achievements and the good deeds that you do. Make friends, and enjoy your moments with them.

I started my first semester at SUNY Buffalo in January 1982. Since it was called the "spring semester," I thought all the cold weather and snow would be over by the end of March. And I wouldn't freeze on my twenty-minute walk to the campus. Boy! What a mistake. It even snowed in May when I was taking my finals. It was a brutal winter. I never felt this cold in my life. Of course, throughout the winter I learned that Buffalo is pretty famous in the United States. The people I met would ask me why on earth I chose Buffalo. I had my first encounter with freezing rain in Buffalo. I understood what lake-effect snow was about. It really snowed in blankets. There were days I had to lift my leg up as high as my belly in order to walk. You could easily get stuck in the hip-high snow. And, believe me it was very tiring. I chose to concentrate on school: study hard, finish, and get out of there.

With limited nutrition and lots of energy spent walking to the school in the snow, I started to fade away. I kept losing weight, and I had no energy left. This lasted for about two years.

We ended up buying a car during the summer of 1982, a year after we arrived. Our first car was a yellow Opel Manta. It was already partially rusted. It lasted pretty long despite my abusing it while trying to take care of it. As with any cars in Buffalo, it was rotting away from salt in the winter. So, one day I bought a can of car paint. That was a pretty big investment for me. I started to spray over the rusty spots. And not knowing at all how to do it the right way, I pressed the nozzle and sprayed all over without covering the headlights. At least I made my friends laugh for having yellow-painted headlights.

My dissertation advisor, Dr. Colin Drury, was a well-known researcher in ergonomics. Because of him, his human factors program had a good national reputation. He was a great professor, very friendly, but with a temper that could be heard in the form of heavy footsteps when he was walking up the stairs to his office. If we heard those temper-laden footsteps, all of us, his students, would rush to our offices and close our doors to avoid being the first victim of his temper. He was very smart, creative, and fun to work with. There were eight of us doing graduate studies with him. Besides me, there were three Americans, one Sri Lankan, two Indians, one Taiwanese, and one Chinese. We had a great group.

I see my Buffalo friends once in a while at conferences. Last time we were all together was at a conference in Orlando. Dr. Drury took us to a really nice Italian restaurant, and we ate and drank for hours. After finishing five or six bottles of wine, you can imagine how memories come back and you celebrate those years together. My Sri Lankan friend, Ravi, currently at Hong Kong University, and I used to sing Beatles' songs at every party we had in Buffalo. Another dear friend, Bishu, teaches at the University of Nebraska at Lincoln.

The department always had wine and cheese parties on Friday afternoons for the faculty and graduate students. Of course the faculty would join us only for an hour, and then they would go home. We, the hungry bunch, would stay for hours finishing all the cheese, crackers, and cheap Chablis. Our department secretary, Lucy, always joined us. She was a colorful, cheerful person with many talents. She was part of a professional belly dancing group. Once she invited us to a Lebanese restaurant where she occasionally danced. We had a big table of twenty students and danced all night.

The first semester I did well on my grades. This led to my first real job in the United States: teaching assistant. I finally had an income and a real responsibility, taking care of seventy undergraduate students. It was a great feeling to be able to afford my own textbooks rather than borrowing the old editions from the library. The assistantship was going to start in September with the fall semester, but we had some savings and managed not to starve during the summer. We could afford to go to McDonald's once a month. And we even managed to go to two restaurants. The first one was a typical American restaurant, and the second one was a Chinese restaurant.

My First Restaurant Experience

In the 1980s all average American restaurants used to serve the same food. The new era of creative cooking was not here yet. The menus usually consisted of steak, pork chops, trout almondine, broiled or fried chicken, linguini with alfredo sauce, beef stroganoff, hamburger, and surf and turf (steak and lobster tail—an expensive choice). And I was not aware at that time that the waiters were good at interrogating the customer about what he or she wanted to order. They would present a series of options. I had no idea what they were about. Knowing how limited my conversational English was, I decided to choose the easiest and the cheapest dish: hamburger. I thought that was all I had to say, and I could say hamburger easily. The conversation between the waiter and I went like this:

"How would you like your hamburger done?"

"Cooked."

"I mean, would you like it rare (I thought that meant it is hard to find), medium rare (that is easier to find than rare), medium, or well done?" From my experience in Turkey, you cook meat really well so that you do not get sick.

"Well done. Burned." Later I learned that the cows were slaughtered in the United States by electrocuting them, and this way the blood stays in the body. That grossed me out. I still cannot eat meat if the blood is oozing out when I cut it. This is the reason I did not go to medical school: I cannot look at blood.

"Would you like soup or salad?"

"Salad." I wish I said soup.

"What would you like as a dressing?" How do you dress a plate of salad? Clothes? I was imagining putting a hat and a scarf on the tomatoes, carrots, and lettuce pieces. She guessed I had no knowledge of salad dressing:

"Blue cheese, Italian, Thousand Island, or French?"

I still didn't know what dressing was; so I opted for blue cheese. At least I knew what blue cheese was.

"Would you like french fries, mashed potatoes, or baked potato?" No idea what french fries were. Later during dinner I kind of guessed what they were by checking the other tables.

"Baked potato" I said. This was the most comprehensible choice.

"Would you like sour cream or butter?" Oh my God! When is this going to end?

"Nothing!"

"Nothing at all?" She was surprised.

"Thank you. That is all."

And then she turned to your dad. Here we go again. I am hungry. I just want food. I wish they had a cheat-sheet with the menu for the first-timers.

Slowly, I learned the restaurant customs in the United States. I learned to say: salad, Italian dressing, baked potato naked, and "medium done" meat. I learned that "well done" means totally dried out meat, which was not good at all. And the salad came before dinner. That was my first lesson in learning the order of food arrival at the table in the United States.

Now the restaurants are fun to eat at. There are hundreds of salad varieties—from curried roasted pear, walnut and arugula salads to baby spinach with pomegranate infused dressing. You do not have to answer all those questions, and it is incredible to find so many varieties with great flavors.

At least I did not have to make choices at McDonald's. For a while, the only thing I asked for was no ice in the Coke. Coming from Turkey, where there were no ice in drinks that time, I found it very unusual to see the cups filled with ice with a little bit of drink in them. Especially in winter, I could not imagine drinking water with ice. Forget about ice cream in winter. But now I eat ice cream year round and I love it. During those first years, ice cream was a treat for us. I would buy that typical ice cream container with strawberry, chocolate, and vanilla in it. We would savor the box for many days until the ice cream started to taste like the cardboard it came in.

That winter of 1982 was brutal for me. I was missing my family like crazy and suffering from the cold and the snow, studying hard, and learning a new culture. I cried almost every night. But it still never occurred to me to go back to Turkey. I was not going to be a failure!

There was a Greek store close to our house. I would cherish everything in the store that reminded me of Turkish cuisine, especially feta cheese, filo dough to make *börek* (spinach, cheese, or meat pie), preserved grape leaves to make *dolma* (stuffed grape leaves), olives, and jam.

My favorite meal is breakfast, and especially a Turkish breakfast: boiled eggs, a variety of cheeses (feta, *kaşar, hellim, tulum,* string, etc.), jams with no pectin (quince, strawberry, sour cherry, rose petal, apricot, baby figs, orange rind, and blackberry). In Turkey, the jams are usually made with fruit, water, sugar, and lemon juice. So the jams are not too thick, but just thick enough to spread on the bread. Then the olives: oil-cured wrinkly, shiny, ebony olives, and cracked and cured small green olives bursting with flavor. This is my dream weekend breakfast. I also learned to love ricotta cheese (especially fresh ricotta) spread on toasted bread instead of butter. I add a nice Turkish tea or a cup of herbal tea to my breakfast.

Places I Lived in Buffalo

During my Buffalo years, from September 1981 until May 1984, I lived at seven different addresses.

The first one was the one on Allenhurst Road, about a twenty-five-minute walking distance to the campus. It was a two-story, two-bedroom garden apartment. We shared it with two Turkish friends who we knew from Turkey, who graduated just a year before us from the same department in METU. They were just friends then and ended up getting married. We were married then and ended up getting divorced. The garden apartment was in a group of similar apartments all connected in rows, with the tenants mostly graduate students from all over the world. We stayed there for only two months. Then we moved to the small apartment only a block away. This one, again, was in an apartment development complex that rented out to students. We were on the first floor. It had one bedroom, a small living room, and a large kitchen. This was the apartment where we spent our first dreadful winter.

When we bought our Opel Manta in 1982, we explored more possibilities and ended up moving to an old apartment building with big bay windows. It was well insulated and heat was included in the rent. And they kept the heat pretty high. It was a relief to sleep in just pajamas rather than three layers of sweaters, and even be able to open windows in winter to get some fresh air. This was on Kenmore Avenue. There was a movie theater just across from us, almost a magical place. It was a very old theater with beautiful red velvet curtains and soft chairs. It had probably not been renovated for ages. Everything was falling apart. It felt like the 1960s movie theaters. It played all the classics, which changed every week: *Casablanca, Gaslight, Citizen Kane, Gone with the Wind,* and others. I had a chance to see all the classics for a dollar each. However, it all ended after a few months. The theater was demolished, and a new shopping center was built in its space. What a shame.

After settling down in this new apartment, we started inviting people for dinner. Since we had more money coming from my assistantship, we could afford giving modest dinner parties. Our first guests were my professor Dr. Drury and his wife, my dissertation co-advisor Dr. Sara Czaja and her husband, and your dad's dissertation advisor Dr. Babu. I did not have enough utensils for seven people so I had to go to a Goodwill store. I bought forks and knives for twenty-five cents each and a couple of plates for fifty cents. We served Turkish food: *köfte, börek*, Turkish green beans, and Turkish salad. We also had *rakı*. Dr. Drury was very happy and very friendly. I thought about slipping *rakı* in his morning coffee to temper his mood.

When Christmas came, one of the graduate students, the oldest among us—he had a seven-year-old child and a baby on the way—gave all of us Christmas ornaments. We all received three beautiful little glass bells nested together that gave a very delicate sound. I kept that ornament for many years in its box, until I could hang it on our first Christmas tree in 1991. I still have it and cherish it every year. You know how it is when you are putting the tree up every year; you go down a memory lane for each ornament.

The winter of 1983 came, harsh again. This time, I could not decide which was worse, driving or walking in the blizzard. It was snow after snow. The most watched program became the weather news. The last traces of snow finally disappeared at the end of May. Although it was very hard work, those days were good days with my friends. We had the same goal: to obtain a higher education and to strive for success. My goal was still to go back to my university in Ankara and live in those houses.

Your dad defended his dissertation in the spring of 1983. After his defense, he started to get ready for the next chapter in his life. He already had an offer from Pratt Institute. I started looking for a cheap room for myself in the summer. Given that I would not be earning money during the summer months, we would be having trouble going through summer with the little savings we had. I found a room at an old lady's house. There was another girl renting the second bedroom upstairs. We shared a bath.

One early morning in June we took another turn in our lives. Your dad and I drove to New York City to rent a place for him. It was our first trip to New York City. We put all his belongings into our Opel Manta. We took my belongings to a friend's house for storage until my move later when I returned from New York. The car was pretty loaded with your dad's clothes, books, a sleeping bag, a pillow, and some kitchen items. When we came close to the city, we thought it would be easy to follow the map, cross over Manhattan and go to Brooklyn. I was trying to figure out the map. It was impossible with all the intersecting highways. We ended up on the FDR Drive on the east side of Manhattan going seventy-five miles an hour. I had no idea what the exits meant, and your dad kept asking me what to do next. I was petrified. I am a planner you know; I studied the map for days before our trip. I had a specific road to take, and there was no way of finding it when you got on the wrong road. After several minutes, which seemed like hours, we ended up finding the entry to the Brooklyn Bridge. Even in that commotion, the magnitude of the city and the beauty of the bridge struck me. I never forgot that day. After that incident, I never drove to the city.

We ended up at the Pratt Institute around two in the afternoon. It was a Friday in June. The school was literally empty. Your dad had not notified his new department that he was coming. There was no housing arrangement. He went inside to find somebody, and I was supposed to call these numbers we found in the New York Times rental section. While marking the numbers to call, I fell asleep. I was upset that I fell asleep. But later we realized, even if I had not fallen asleep, we would not be able to find an apartment or a room in New York City in two hours and move in. I don't know what we were thinking. How crazy it was to drive to New York and expect to find a rental room in a couple of hours. None of the places we called that evening worked out. We ended up getting a hotel right next to the Brooklyn Bridge, on the Brooklyn side. I don't remember the name, but it looked like one of those filthy hotels where crack addicts stayed. I was hoping to take a shower at least, after the long drive on a hot summer day, but there was no hope. The bathtub was filled with cockroaches. They were everywhere. The sheets were filled with stain marks. For a price of thirty-five dollars a night, I should have known not to assume anything. We had very little money. Even thirty-five dollars was hurting us. But, it hurt even more to pay that amount to spend the night with cockroaches. We stayed there only one night. But the next day was no better. Spending all morning and afternoon searching, we finally found a room for 200 dollars a month. It was a tiny room with a tiny window. There were mouse droppings on the linoleum floor, which had an unidentified color of dirt and grime. The cockroaches were everywhere. I broke down and cried, feeling bad for your dad and how he had to live there. That night I left, still not showered for three days and still smelly, tired, and upset. I took a bus back to Buffalo. It was my first trip on the Short Line bus that runs between Olean, New York and New York City. I remember that day. The bus driver stopped at a store to get lottery tickets. I did not even have a spare dollar to buy one.

On Monday, Pratt found a studio apartment for your dad. I wish we had waited until Monday to come to the city. He ended up moving out of that tiny room and could not get his first month's rent back, which was a whopping 200 dollars.

I continued working on my dissertation in Buffalo in July, and visited your dad in August.

I rented a room at an old lady's house during that summer. When I rented the place the owner's brother warned me that it was his sister's house and she had mental illness. She occupied the downstairs area, and another girl rented a bedroom upstairs. I was allowed to use the kitchen to cook and was given a half shelf in the refrigerator to put my food on. I was also allowed to watch television in the living room. That never worked out though. The old lady would stare at me for hours if I sat in the same room with her. I was scared for the three months that I stayed there. Actually, she was a very nice lady.

I studied every night until about one or two in the morning. Unfortunately it was summer, the window was always open, and one crow dedicated himself to be my unwanted alarm clock at five in the morning. He would perch on the lonely little tree in the front yard and start crowing. There was no way I could sleep when he was doing his morning ritual. I started to carry stones into my room, and whenever he crowed I would throw stones at him from my little window. Of course, I missed him every time. The stones would make him go away for about twenty minutes or so, and I would dose off again only to be awakened for the next round. I wonder if he thought that the stones were used as a snooze button!

Those were very busy but quiet days for me. I was working on my dissertation. Once in a while I would visit my friends for dinner or tea. I literally had no money. With New York being so costly for your dad, there was no money for me. I used to buy a box of spaghetti and a small bottle of ketchup. That would be my dinner for three nights. At least it was summer and I did not pay for utilities.

When fall came, with the assistantship salary restarting, I moved to an upstairs apartment with two other girls. It was a beautiful apartment with all wood trim and big windows. I had to borrow furniture from my friends—including a smelly twin mattress with no box spring. We carried the mattress on top of my friend's car in the rain. And the mattress was wet for about a month.

January 1984 was another moving month for me. This time to Alfred, New York in the Finger Lakes region, close to Route 17 that runs across the entire state.

8

My Teaching Years

In the fall of 1983, your dad was teaching at Pratt Institute and I was working hard on my dissertation. Then, an opportunity came for us to teach at the same university. Your dad and I had an interview together at Alfred University in Alfred, New York. Alfred was two hours south of Buffalo. They needed faculty for their brand new industrial engineering department. The first person hired was one of the Ph.D. candidates from SUNY Buffalo, Wilfred, who was a friend of your dad. It was a good starting job for us since we knew that having no "stars on our shoulders" yet in terms of research and teaching experience, we were lucky that we could go and work at the same place together. I agreed to start in the spring semester, January 1984, before my dissertation was completed. And your dad would start in September 1984, after his year at Pratt would end. I thought driving to Buffalo for two hours every week would be no problem. And, here again, I forgot the lake-effect snow.

I realize now how much I had committed to that time. I was a brand new professor with three brand new courses to prepare and a dissertation to complete. I had to prepare lecture notes for three courses, and review those notes at least three times before my lectures. In the meantime, my dissertation was going full speed and I had to spend at least four days in Buffalo. I commuted back and forth between Alfred and Buffalo: juggling to finish my dissertation and teach for the first time.

I moved out of the shared apartment at the beginning of January. I went to Alfred in December to find an apartment. The snow was piling up everywhere. I was walking to the engineering building in the campus and realized I chose the worst possible place for me. I am petrified of dogs and Alfred had a no-leash policy. Dogs were wandering around freely. One of them somehow smelled my fear and started to run towards me. I did my best to shoo him away. I was hopeless and helpless. All of a sudden, I saw a car coming and jumped in front of it. I begged the driver, who was laughing at the strange scene of an all-bundled-up woman running away from a dog, to take me in. He turned out to be the ceramic art department chair. After that day, for four years, I always watched my back for any dog presence. I changed my routes just to avoid them. These dogs would even walk into the classrooms. And I had my share of that in one of my classes. I really embarrassed myself once, hiding behind a chair when a large dog wandered into the classroom checking up on his owner, one of my students.

After staying with our friends for two weeks, I rented a small, two-bedroom apartment in Almond, New York, only five miles from Alfred. Since the university paid for the moving expenses from my place in Buffalo to Almond, I hired a moving company. Two men with a huge truck came on a freezing day in January. The company assumed I had a house full of furniture—all I had was one single room. My belongings, all I collected from September 1981 until January 1984 from curbsides to garage sales, filled only one-tenth of the truck. They took my plants too. Unfortunately, all my plants died from freezing during the move.

That year was one of the hardest times in my life in terms of work. I worked nonstop, round the clock, in two locations, with high demands from both sides.

Thankfully, the dean at Alfred University helped me have my courses scheduled on Mondays and Tuesdays. I would teach one class Monday morning, one class Tuesday morning, and then I would either drive or catch a bus to Corning to teach another class to graduate students from Corning Glass. My class in Corning would start at six and end at nine at night. Then, I would eat a quick dinner. If I drove to Corning, I would drive back to Almond and then would take a bus to Buffalo the next morning. If I took the bus, then I would catch a bus to Buffalo from Corning. I would arrive in Buffalo right before midnight and take a taxi to my friend Bishu's house, where I was renting a room to use during my trips to Buffalo. I started to use this room less and less, since I was staying up all night at the department to get my experiments ready. Dr. Drury gave me a key to the subject preparation room, where they had a medical bed. I would crawl into the bed around four in the morning and would leave a note to the cleaners to wake me up around seven before they left the building. I had great friends. They would bring me coffee, bagels, and donuts, just to make sure I ate. I would stay in Buffalo until Saturday and go back to Alfred to prepare my lecture notes for the following week.

The whole cycle was brutal: teaching Mondays and Tuesdays until late, going to Buffalo, spending Wednesdays, Thursdays, Fridays, and Saturdays at the department working on my dissertation almost twenty hours a day; going back to Alfred late Saturday night, and prepare my lecture notes all day Sunday for the next week. To this very hectic schedule, add the snow, ice storms, and cold. And this lasted until the end of April.

I just want to tell you of one incident. One very cold February night, after my Corning class, I went to a nearby restaurant to eat and then catch the bus to Buffalo. However, my watch was incorrect, and I missed the bus by two minutes. I was stuck in Corning, with no place to go, and it was freezing outside. There was a taxi stand next to the bus stop. I calculated in my head that if I found a place to stay in Corning, I would have the same issue the next morning. So I negotiated a price with one of the taxi drivers to take me to Almond. Just as we got off one of the highways, the taxi broke down. There was no way to stay in the taxi more than thirty minutes without any heat, and there were no cars passing. The driver told me to stay in the taxi and he would walk to the gas station, about two miles back to get some help. There were no mobile phones at that time. I was debating in my head whether to walk with him with my dressy shoes on or sit in the taxi facing a freeze or other consequences for being all alone late at night in a taxi. It was eleven at night. Just then, my luck turned. A bus showed up! This was the bus, which I totally forgot about, that runs very late between Corning and Alfred. I jumped in front of the bus. No matter what, I was not going to let the bus go without me. I paid the taxi driver and jumped on the bus. The bus driver was kind enough to give the taxi driver a lift to a gas station.

I remember a similar incident, years later, in July 1998, in Japan. After flying thousands of miles, changing trains and buses, I was in a remote region in Japan going to a conference at Shonan Village Center, in the city of Kanagawa. Here were the directions I received from the conference center:

1. At Tokyo Airport take JR Narita Express.—After the long flight it took forty-five minutes to go through the customs, buy a train ticket, go down several levels of the train station and find the right platform.

2. Change at Yokohama station to JR Yokosuka Line.—This was not easy, carrying a suitcase and a laptop.
3. Get off at Zushi station.—After about a two-hour ride, I did this fine.
4. From JR Zushi station take Keikyu bus no. 16.—I had the name of the place, and the bus number written on a piece of paper, both in Japanese and in English. And I showed my paper to three people getting on the bus to be sure it was the right bus to go to Shonan Village Center. They all nodded.
5. Get off at Shonan Kokusaimura Center Mae.—Well, I did not reach there that easily.

After about fifteen minutes on the bus, I felt uneasy. Something was telling me that I was on the wrong bus. I yelled out, "Does anyone know English?" No response. "Does anyone know Turkish?" This really was stretching hope. No response. After a few minutes a high school student with pretty good English came and sat next to me. Within seconds, I was informed that I was on the wrong bus. No, there were no hotels in the destination where I was going. Nope. There were no taxis to take me from one point to another. He said I could get off at the fork where the road splits. The bus was taking the right side of the fork. I was supposed to be going to the left. There was a little bus stop shelter, and it was pitch dark. Nobody knew if there were any late buses. My watch said 10 p.m. I started to accept my situation: just sit on my suitcase for another eight hours until I get a ride. What I did not know was that the student was getting off the bus at the same stop as I did. About two minutes later, a sleek BMW stopped. A gorgeous Japanese woman with perfect English offered me a ride to the conference center. The student who helped me was sitting in the passenger seat. In about thirty minutes, I was in my hotel room ready to jump into the shower after a long journey to a place that will always be in my memory.

My courses and my dissertation took all my time until April of 1984. When the weather was just becoming mild, I completed my biggest milestone: I defended my dissertation. One of my advisors gave a big party at her house that night. Your dad came from New York. The next day I took him to the bus station to take a bus back to New York. He had another month there to finish the semester and move to Almond. We would be back together again. I drove that morning to Almond. It was a Saturday morning. I had to prepare my lecture notes for my Monday and Tuesday classes. That was nothing compared to the many months of sleepless nights. I was done.

After your dad left Pratt Institute, he joined me at Alfred University. We left Almond and we moved to Hornell. It was a slightly larger town than Almond. It had the major stores! K-Mart, Pizza Hut, Friendly's, a typical American restaurant, a Chinese restaurant, a bar, and a lovely little restaurant that prepared the most amazing creative meals. That was it. There were a couple of clothing stores still surviving. The downtown looked like a movie set, where the tumble weeds rolled down the streets, and where the stores were all boarded up. The town was not doing well at all—turning from a bustling town with a railroad station and a couple of factories to a ghost town with almost no industry or farms to support it.

Well, we spent about three years there. We learned all the basics of American town living—away from the university culture. We had a great time with our landlords, the Palmer family. They taught us barbecuing, fly fishing, boating, gardening, camping at Thousand Islands, renting a cottage at Finger Lakes, and going to local fairs to eat five strawberry shortcakes after the Fourth of July beer drinking. We moved out of Hornell at the end of the summer of 1987, back to Almond.

A few months later, in January, you were born. I took you to Turkey in May right after the commencement at Alfred University. And at the end of the summer of 1988, after we came back from Turkey, we moved from Almond to Washington, D.C. to my new job at George Washington University. Our lives, yet again, were drastically changed. The year in Washington, D.C. was one of my hardest years, physically and emotionally.

After we came back from being pampered in Turkey with good food and good company from all of my family, we flew back to the loneliness one more time. This time was even harder: a new job for me, an eight-month old baby, and a new place. And I was going to do this all by myself. This was another point in my life where I just jumped in without thinking how hard it would be. I knew we would manage it somehow, and I was hoping that things would get into gear and keep functioning. Well, it really did not turn out that way.

Washington, D.C., Chicken Pox, and Illnesses Galore

When we came back from Turkey, we drove to Washington, D.C. to find a place to rent. We had no idea how expensive the rents would be compared to where we came from. We were only paying 300 dollars rent for that big house in Almond. And we thought for 500 dollars or a bit more we could get a decent two-bedroom apartment. So, we started with that limit, and all the apartments we saw within that range were infested with cockroaches and were in unsafe neighborhoods for you and me. We ended up renting an apartment in a high-rise building in Alexandria, Virginia. The rent was much more than we anticipated. After settling in the apartment, I spent a few days looking for a daycare for you. All the daycares I could afford were full. I wait-listed you at the KinderCare, a thirty-minute drive south of our apartment. And while waiting for that, I found a lady who took care of babies at her home. That did not work out well, but luckily KinderCare had an opening for your age group.

So, while I was going to teach in Washington, your dad still had the teaching job at Alfred University. He was going to have to juggle teaching his classes at Alfred in New York and spending time with us in D.C. Fortunately, he was able to arrange for his classes to be finished by Wednesday, and he would drive to D.C. to spend time with us until Sunday afternoon. I was alone at least half the week.

Amid all this commotion, I realized that my clothes were not fit for a chic Washington, D.C. crowd. Here I was coming from upstate New York farmland, where carrying a rifle at the back of your pickup truck often piled up with fishing equipment or dirt for your garden was the norm. And you don't need fancy clothes teaching at a university that is miles away from any city. So I just had jeans, a couple pairs of slacks, shirts, and sweaters. I did not even have decent shoes. I had to spend two days at a mall buying reasonably acceptable clothes. You cannot turn a farm girl into a chic city girl in one day, but you can turn a professor from a farmland into a professor in a city pretty quickly. That was the best part of teaching.

I was ready for the challenges of our new lives in Washington, D.C. I knew it was going to be very hard. I was ready to take care of you, to succeed as an associate professor at George Washington University, and to manage driving in and around D.C. But, I was not ready for what was coming. You always had sleep problems when you were a baby. I could not get you to sleep early. If I succeeded having you asleep by eight at night, you would then wake up at midnight and stay up until three or four in the morning. Juggling between working on my research and preparing my lecture notes after you were in bed, I was not able to sleep until midnight anyway. So my sleeping pattern just became from four until seven in the morning. This lasted almost an entire year. With all these changes, a new daycare and sleep problems, you started to get sick. Really sick. We spent many hours at the hospital getting tests done. I drove you to the Children's Hospital emergency room a couple of times. The hospital was miles away and I had to drive through a tough neighborhood in the middle of the night. They could not identify what was wrong with you. You were just melting away with fever, diarrhea, and throwing up. You lost pound after pound. You could not even hold up your head. I was frantic. We went to see many doctors. You were poked everywhere for blood tests. They could not find a cure for you.

This lasted three months, until spring came. Then you started to eat and play. You started to have color on your cheeks. Then, as if you did not go through enough hard times, further problems developed. Right at the time of the famous Cherry Blossom Festival, you dislocated your arm while playing. We took you to the emergency room. Yes, the problem was solved with a little twist by the emergency doctor, but you caught chicken pox there. I could not leave the house for five days. I could not take you out. Chicken pox was everywhere on your body, including inside your eyes. I was out of food. We started to eat the same food: your baby food from jars. We knew nobody to get us any help. One day, at the peak of the cherry blossoms, I could not stay in the house one more day with a sick child. I wrapped you up completely so that no one could see that you had chicken pox, and drove directly to the Tidal Basin in D.C. I stopped the car next to a cherry tree. I got out and felt the April warmth for the first time after days of being inside. I put my face into the blossoms. I cried and cried.

My Driving in D.C.

I remember one of the jokes my mom used to say. "Do you know any crazy person?" she used to ask. When someone said, "No", she said, "Haven't you seen a mother with a baby?" That was me in D.C.

What on earth made me move to D.C. to teach at a university located in the middle of a crowded city, and then to travel on the highways and byways every day to reach a daycare that closed at 6:30 p.m.? Especially since two days a week my classes were ending at exactly 5:50 p.m. I had to run to my car and drive to Route 395. I had to be at the Route 395 HOV (High Occupancy Vehicle) express lanes entry point exactly at 6 p.m. Not a minute less or a minute more. That was when they lifted the ban on cars with one person. The police at the entrance of the express lanes would force me to go to the regular lanes, which were already bumper to bumper. I had to be in the express lanes to make it to the daycare on time, and the minute they opened the express lanes, I would be one of the first cars zooming through. I always made the daycare right before 6:30 p.m. The daycare would have only one light on: the light in the director's room. She would be waiting for me with you on her lap. There was no one else left. And my night would start all over again. We would go home and I would feed you, give you a bath, play with you, and listen to some music. And pray for you to go to sleep early, which never happened. Your main entertainment at that time was to turn the light switches on and off. This would last about two hours a day. Here I was holding you in my arms for two hours, as if I had a nice calm day, still with images of my daily mad dash to get you from the daycare.

I was a single mom, a crazy woman, and a career woman trying to do her best to raise you.

9

Moving to New Jersey

After realizing that we could not stay in two states while raising you, I applied and was accepted for a position at AT&T Bell Laboratories in Whippany, New Jersey. Your dad had already accepted a position at Rutgers University.

My nightmare year in Washington, D.C. was now behind me. We moved to New Jersey. After staying at a hotel for a few weeks, we moved to a townhouse in Morris Plains, just off of Route 10. Route 10 was this long, never-ending highway with shopping plazas on both sides, speckled with a few good restaurants, but mostly with prominent fast food chains.

After the hectic Washington D.C. year, this was a great relief. I really did not even mind the extra driving. Although we lived only five minutes away from my office building, I had to drive every day forty-five minutes north to drop you off at your daycare, and then drive back forty-five minutes south to work. And believe me, just like any other New Jersey location, there were at least four alternative routes to get to the daycare and come back.

Aside from all the driving, I was pretty happy with the new corporate life. It was different from teaching and doing research. The politics were different. Somehow, I enjoyed it.

We stayed in Morris Plains less than a year. I changed my job within AT&T, and we moved to Freehold, New Jersey. We lived at the Poets Corner townhouse development. Two townhouses shared a wall, and each one had a nice gated patio entry. That is where I met my friend Toni (short for Antoinette). Her husband was from Ethiopia. Her house was the one attached to ours. Her son and you became fast friends. There were two other boys in our cul-de-sac of about twelve townhomes. You were always out playing. It was so cute to watch you all. Four three-year-old boys do a lot of mischief and get into a lot of mud. On Halloween nights, we mothers used to walk you around the townhouse complex for trick or treat. Your costumes evolved over time, from a pumpkin to a firefighter to a policeman to Dracula.

Our First Real Christmas with Our First Christmas Tree

Do you remember your first Christmas tree? You came back from daycare one day, just four years old, crying. That heart-breaking kind of cry, not the temper tantrum one. "Why don't we have a Christmas tree?", in between sobs, "Everyone at the school has one." We had to make a decision then, which was not that hard, whether to treat the Christmas tree as a religious thing or a holiday symbol. Before we left Turkey, I remember there were Noel trees sold. Although more than ninety-five percent of Turks are Muslims, there were still Noel tree buyers. There were not many, but they included diplomats, foreigners, and some Turks who wanted to have some holiday decorations for the New Year. In Turkey, the presents were always given on New Year's Eve. Father Noel (Noel Baba), aka Santa Claus, came on New Year's Eve in my country.

Your dad and I decided that we would treat the Christmas tree as a symbol of celebrating the New Year and creating a festive mood in the house. Why not? After the New Year, we would be facing a dreadful winter anyway. So we went to look for a Christmas tree on the night of December 23. We found one store that had two left—the sickliest ones that no one would buy. We bought the better of the two. At the same store, we found a tree stand that we still use today, just one set of string lights, and a dozen ornaments. Those were the first decorations for our first Christmas tree. After we decorated it, you asked where we could get an angel for the tree top. Well, we did not have an angel. I put your glowworm on top as our angel. He was very cute on top. You had to give up sleeping with him for a couple of weeks. After that day, you and I started our quest for ornaments and lights, which lasted for several years. Now, we have a beautifully decorated tree every year. And I should thank you for that. I love Christmas trees. They have a soothing effect on me. Just turn the room lamps off and watch the flickering lights play wonders on the ornaments.

Strawberries and Champagne

I really enjoyed living in Freehold. It was close to all the horse farms and farm stands. Every June, my friend Toni and I would pile our kids in a car and take them strawberry picking in Colts Neck. We would eat half the berries we picked, and bring the rest home to make strawberry topping or jam. One warm Saturday in June, Toni decided to plant flowers on her patio. She asked me to help her. I told her that the only way to get through a planting process on a hot summer day would be with strawberries and champagne. We had our three stops that morning. We picked strawberries, we bought dozens of plants, and we bought champagne. We took our champagne glasses, poured ice-cold champagne, and then filled them with fresh strawberries. I don't know how, but we ended up planting everything we bought and had a great time doing it.

Family and Friends

The summer of 1991 was extremely hectic. First, my brother and his wife Özden came. My brother had a three-month residency at the Cleveland Clinic in Ohio. They flew to New York, stayed with us a few days, and then we drove them to Cleveland. After three months, they came back to New Jersey and I arranged our first Caribbean trip. Since they only had a visa for entry to the United States, I had to choose one of the United States Virgin Islands. I chose St. Thomas. It was right after a hurricane. Part of the island had been devastated. We stayed there four days. My brother, your Mehmet Dayı, declared that he was the first Turkish man on the beach who brought *rakı* to St. Thomas. He constantly played with you. You loved going in the water and playing with the waves. Your Mehmet Dayı even pretended being a walrus by sticking pencils in his nose. It was so hard to say goodbye to them. A few days after my brother and Özden left, my parents visited us. This was my dad's second (first one was in 1963) and my mom's first trip to the United States. We took them to Niagara Falls, Alfred, Hornell, Almond, and Dansville. There is a picture of you, with my parents in the background, rolling in the grass in front of the Nicholas H. Noyes Hospital in Dansville where you were born. It was a hot summer day, and the hospital looked really different than the last time I saw it on a cold January day. Then we drove to Toronto and then to the Thousand Islands at the St. Lawrence River. Your dad and I used to camp there when we were at Alfred University.

My First House and the Divorce

It was the summer of 1993. Your dad's best friend Necati, his wife Ayla, and one of their daughters, Bahar, were visiting us. They are the ones who gave Tornado to you as a present. While they were staying with us, Necati and Ayla took Bahar to Disney World. While they were away, one August day, I got a call from one of my close friends, Pat, that a few of our friends were going out to lunch. We were all in that giant AT&T building in Holmdel. We had a wonderful lunch in Sea Bright, right on the Navesink River. That is when Karen, another friend at the table, told me that she just bought a townhouse in Holmdel, and that the price was incredibly good. Holmdel had a lot of "McMansions" that I could not afford. I always wanted you to go to the Holmdel schools. After lunch, I snuck out to the K. Hovnanian sales office by the townhouse development. They had no end units left. So, I put our name on the list. We were 320th on the list of people wanting an end-unit townhouse. I waited a couple of days.

It was Friday. Necati, Ayla, and Bahar were coming back from Disney World that day. I was still at work. I called the sales office and asked if there was any hope to get an end unit, otherwise I was thinking about getting one of the middle units. The sales agent said that she had received a call from one of the end-unit buyers. He was backing out of the sale due to his job transfer. The unit was available! If I had not called that day, the sales agent was going to go through the waiting list.

"This is your lucky day," she said. "Do you want it?" I told her that I wanted to see the model unit and talk to my husband. So Saturday morning we, including Necati, Ayla and Bahar, drove to see the model townhouse. And I fell in love. Ayla and Necati encouraged me to get the house. I took the first step and filled out a loan application that day.

From August until February, I often went to the construction site to see my house being built. I saw them putting in the windows, doors, kitchen cabinets, deck, and much more. I walked through a foot of mud just to peek in through the kitchen patio door to see how the place looked. I got chased by the developers many times.

The day before we moved, I completed the closing process and got the key. I invited several friends that night to come and celebrate our new house before we moved in. About twenty of us had pizza, wine, and beer in the empty, brand new house. I was so happy. My heart was racing, realizing that this was my first house. Well the truth was, like many people say, the bank owned it. But it didn't matter. It was my house. One of my friends had a bottle of champagne. He shook the bottle a bit too much. I ended up with champagne stains all over the floor. We cleaned up most of the stains, except for a few on the green marble around the fireplace. I remembered that night of my celebration for the next thirteen years every time I dusted the marble.

And then the moving day came. It was not at all what I dreamed it to be. I had hired movers, just two men and a truck. I was hoping to start early so we could finish early. I planned to go to Macaroni Grill that night and enjoy warm pasta. What else could have been better, pasta on a cold February night after a long moving day? That is all I wanted that day.

Unfortunately, the moving day was one of my nightmares. We had a big snowstorm that night after the party. The moving company called in the morning and told us that they could not shovel the truck out of its location. We ended up renting a U-Haul and moved everything ourselves. I hired my neighbor Toni's son, who helped a little, but not until the end of the move. I left you with Toni, but she only kept you until early afternoon. So, you had to go back and forth with us with this small U-Haul truck. The last trip was at 1 a.m., we were hardly keeping our eyelids open. You were sitting on my lap, still awake. Every speck of snow was frozen. I had a bag of dried socks that I carried with me all day. I kept changing our socks every hour so our feet would not freeze. We finally went to bed in our new home at 3 a.m., and I never had a chance to eat pasta at Macaroni Grill that night.

We moved to our house in Holmdel on February 14, 1994. Your dad moved out in August 1996, after our split in November 1995. The first two years at the house were very stormy. Every time I think about those early years, I imagine a little six-year-old boy, looking through the bars on the staircase, down to the living room, and listening to the shouting matches that mom and dad were having. Weren't we the ones who were supposed to give you a steady and happy environment? No, we forgot. We forgot how to respect each other. We passed the point of no return and the divorce came. It was a tough one.

Many months and many struggles later, I finally knew it was time to move on. You know, every time you need to make a decision, it is best to do it with your heart, not your mind. All those pros and cons are just for you to justify what you want, not what you have to do. If you listen to your heart very carefully, you will know what you want. Don't ever close your eyes to what you feel and what you desire. It is your life anyway. Although I was worried that you would be very upset, and would have a hard time adjusting (maybe never) to the divorce of your parents, I thought it might be better that you did not grow up in a house where bitterness and sadness were the norm.

I remember your reaction when your dad told you that we were getting a divorce. That was it. One sentence was enough to change your life. For two years, you were very angry with me. You suffered a lot. I am really sorry for what happened. I wish I could erase what you went through. I can never forgive myself about many things, especially our divorce. I was very happy not to be with your dad anymore. That must have blinded me not to see your suffering in the meantime.

One November day in 1996, at the Freehold court house, my sixteen-year marriage came to an end. But just like sunshine after a storm, Al came to our lives.

10

AT&T Years and Beyond

My AT&T years were very crucial in my life. I started in August 1989 in Whippany, a military looking building, and then moved to the AT&T Bell Labs building in Holmdel in June 1990. The AT&T building in Holmdel was the largest building that I ever worked in. It housed 6000 employees, and had two restaurants, a bank, a post office, a dry cleaner, and a coffee house. I worked in that building for eight years. I met most of my current friends there. I discovered a large Turkish community, all Bell Labs employees. They were like me, almost the same age, having come to this country to pursue their graduate degrees in different fields. Once in a while we used to get together for lunch. This helped me to adjust to a new community. I was not going from one place to another, and I was not changing jobs. I started to feel that I belonged in New Jersey. We would hold parties at each other's houses. Our kids became friends. I had a chance to become friends with many of my co-workers. Our friendships stayed even after many of us left AT&T, found other jobs, and even moved to other countries. It was easy to do an international party—just invite thirty friends from different countries.

During summer months, all the local summer camp minivans would pull in to the driveways, and we, the parents, would send our kids to camps so that we could work to earn money to pay for the camp. How I wish that I had taken a week off in those years and taken you to beaches or watched movies together. At least we had vacations together, every year, twice a year. I traveled to many places in addition to Turkey every year. Not that I feel guilty about my work, but sometimes I had the utmost desire to be with you on a hot summer day, instead of watching you wave at me from the tiny window of the camp van, with your backpack and your lunch box on your lap. Remember the day that the driver forgot you and another kid at the camp. He had no idea when I asked him where you were. Just as I started to panic, I saw the owner of the camp driving both of you to AT&T.

Those great years went by fast. After AT&T's split, some of our friends moved to Lucent Technologies and stayed at the Holmdel building. We, as AT&T Labs personnel, moved to new building a few miles away in Middletown. I stayed there a couple of years and decided that it was time to move on. With that, my years with AT&T were over. After that, I worked at a consultant company, Human Factors International. Then with the year 2000 bubble burst, I was let go. I had a six-month home stay that I never cherished. I was extremely worried about finding a job which was really hard at that time. I ended up joining Siemens Corporate Research in Princeton, where I stayed for three years as the head of a department. One day, Bob Kerrey, the president of The New School, came to visit our facility at Princeton. With him was the Dean of Parsons School of Design. I had only ten minutes presentation time with them. Within the ten minutes, my department impressed him so much that he wanted to have lunch with us. After lunch, he quietly asked me if I was interested in working for him. I thought he was joking. I received an email from him that night, and about nine months later, I was at The New School, in Manhattan.

11

I Found Love

Just like the sunshine after a storm, when you and I were struggling with the divorce, Al came into our lives. He was not a stranger. I met Al when I first started to work at the AT&T Holmdel building in 1991. He was married. I was married. Our offices were in the same aisle. He was good friends with my co-workers.

Four months after my split with your dad, I went to the Computer-Human Interaction Conference in Vancouver. It was March of 1996. Al was there also. The first day of the conference, a large group of AT&T people went out to dinner. When we came back to the hotel, many of them went to their rooms. Since it was the first time I was out of a house full of pain and bitterness, I wanted to enjoy the feeling of being alive and spending time with my friends. I decided to hang out with Jim Cunningham, my ex-manager, and Bob Mulligan, another manager from the same department. We went to the hotel lobby to have a drink. Al was sitting at the bar having a beer. He was at the Whistler ski resort all day skiing and had just gotten back. He had a glow, a suntan from the mountains. His chameleon eyes were stunning. I am still in love with those eyes. They change color: gray, blue, or green with tiny yellow specks, matching what he wears. He looked different that night. Or, I started to see him differently from that moment on. He joined us at the bar, and we talked for hours. Throughout the conference, there was something there that I had not felt for a long time. I was happy to be with him and with our friends, having lunches and dinners. I left the conference early to go to Los Angeles to attend a Microsoft Tech event. When I reached there, I called my best friend Toni and told her that I was in love. That was it. Many years later, I am still in love. It is that special feeling of being light, happy, hyper, excited; of dreaming away, as if you are on clouds.

At the beginning Al was not on the same page that I was. After the conference I did not see him for several months except on a few business occasions. It took quite a long time for him to see me as a "potential date."

It was the beginning of May, and my team and I went to the AT&T Bell Labs in Murray Hill where Al worked in Greg Blonder's lab. In those times, the Murray Hill lab was the real deep research-oriented lab. That was the time when research was considered valuable for company growth. We had a long meeting, which included lunch. They took us to the nicer restaurant section at the Murray Hill building, where they had a lunch buffet. After getting the food, Al and I sat next to each other. And there was one other person sitting across from us. Al turned and asked me, "Would you like to do something together?" "Do what?" was my answer!

I really did not mean to be smart or witty. But that is what came out of my mouth. He thought that was wacky but cool. I was embarrassed. He said he would call me later. A few days passed and he asked me to a go to the Sting concert at the PNC Bank Art Center. The concert was in July and you would be in Turkey then with your dad. But that did not become our first date. That actually became our sixth or seventh date. The first one was at the end of May. We went to New York on a Saturday. We spent the entire afternoon walking in downtown Manhattan. We stopped to have a cup of coffee in Little Italy and walked some more. At Washington Square Park, a bird pooped on my purse. It was a sign that my luck was changing. We found a great Japanese noodle restaurant and talked and dined over a bottle of wine. Al told me that he was not ready for a serious relationship. He was more into finding a friend to hang out with. Well, we are still hanging out. I love him. You love him, too. This makes me very happy. I love his kids also. I love spending time with them. We always have great fun whenever all our kids are together.

The Sting concert has a special place in our hearts. The day of the concert we packed a backpack with gourmet food and a bottle of wine. Since this was our first concert at the PNC Bank Art Center, we did not know about the food rules. Apparently, we were not allowed to bring in food and drinks. Not just wine, any drinks. I think the only reason is to have us spend our money on the fast food served at the concert. So we decided to eat our gourmet meal on the lawn before the concert. We found a spot where the branches of two trees hugged each other's leaves. We opened our little picnic spread, our red wine, and all the food we brought. Just as we were pouring wine into our glasses, a few drops of rain fell into our wine glasses. It started to rain pretty heavily. Luckily, the tree branches protected us, except for a few drops of rain here and there. It was the most romantic picnic I had with Al. Two people in love, under a tree, with great wine. And the rain drops coming down softly without disturbing us.

We were finished eating just the rain stopped. We walked to the lawn of the concert area. Everyone who went in earlier was soaked. The sky cleared. We spread our blanket. The night fell. And a great concert started.

Six months into our dating, I was feeling more and more attached to Al. He was my savior, my quiet harbor, my friend, and I was deeply into thinking about my life with him. I introduced him to you very slowly. You saw him at several dinner parties along with other friends and started to develop a friendship with him. Al and I worked hard to get ourselves accepted by the kids. First we thought it would be great to introduce ourselves as nonthreatening friends. That is one of the reasons we took a family trip to Turkey, with all of our kids.

First Trip with Al and His Kids

Al and I decided that the best way to get acquainted with each other's kids was to have all of us spend time together at a place that did not belong to any one of us. It was almost like meeting at a place that was not "marked as a territory" by any of us. So we decided to take a trip together. The unanimous choice was Turkey. And believe me; it was not marked at all by me as my territory. Al and his kids Abby (then eighteen) and Nick (then twenty-one) wanted to see my home country. You left early with your dad. At that time you were still good at spending time with your dad, and according to the divorce settlement, both parents would equally share your summer time. Al, Abby, and I left one Friday evening. After we checked our luggage and got our boarding passes, I exclaimed: "Let's have a toast!"

And we drank to "day one." After that day, we drank wine at the end of every evening with a toast to "day x." It was quite a long trip, maybe sixteen or seventeen days. We landed in İstanbul and a car picked us up and took us to the Ayasofya Pensions Hotel. It is a hotel made out of a few "Ottoman" houses. The houses were not really old, they were just built to look like Ottoman houses. Our windows were overlooking the wall of Ayasofya (Hagia Sofia), the famous church built in 537 A.D. by the Byzantine Emperor Justinian, and later turned into a mosque by Sultan Mehmet the Conqueror. Now it is a museum.

While we were settling down in our room, Abby called us in horror, "What the heck is that?" For the first time in her life, she heard *ezan*, the Muslim call for prayer. That is the first time I realized this was their first visit to a country where the majority of the population was Muslim.

We had two full days in İstanbul and did everything that a tourist would do, plus we discovered some additional gems. We ate at Kumkapi, where a row of restaurants serve fresh fish daily. Some of the restaurants have musicians or belly dancing. You need to suffer as you pass the restaurants, constantly bothered by the shouting restaurant workers who are trying to lure you in like a fish. It was an interesting experience, but not the best. It was noisy and colorful. We had good fresh fish, a bit on the expensive side. One day we took the passenger ferry from Eminönü, where the Golden Horn is, all the way to Anadolu Kavağı, the entrance to the Black Sea: that is the entire length of the Bosphorus. The Bosphorus separates the European and the Asian sides of İstanbul. Al and Abby were amazed by the houses on the Bosphorus. The type of these houses is called *yalı,* two- or three-story wooden houses, side by side. Instead of car garages, they have boat garages. Some of them became the victims of "modernization," but there were enough to be stared at with awe. Now they are all under government protection. One of my friends owns one, inherited from her dad. I heard that she needs to get permission even to put a nail in the wall.

The next day we walked to the Topkapı Palace, where we ate lunch like sultans, overlooking the Bosphorus. We toured the underground Basilica Cistern, Ayasofya, and the Grand Bazaar and walked all the way to Eminönü. We took a taxi to İstiklal Street at Beyoğlu. I took them to Saray, one of the oldest dessert shops in İstanbul. We ordered eight or nine items from the menu, each costing a dollar or two. Al and Abby tasted the most spectacular desserts of Turkey for the first time. Abby loved *kazandibi,* burnt milk pudding. After two-and-a-half days of visiting great İstanbul, we flew to İzmir. We had a rental car. We drove an hour in the scorching ninety-plus degrees, constantly playing with the ventilation, trying to get the air conditioner running. Finally we pulled over to the side and realized there was none. No air conditioner for a week of driving in that heat! God bless us. Abby was almost fainting in the back seat. I was constantly wetting a cloth and putting it on Al's neck to keep him awake. We finally arrived at Kuşadası, a beautiful Aegean town very close to Ephesus. We had a reservation at the Kısmet Hotel, one of the oldest hotels in Turkey. The walls were full of pictures of kings and queens who had stayed at the hotel since the early 1900s. With all that traveling, Abby got sick and could not make it to dinner. Al and I, after a sunset dinner in a beautiful garden overlooking the Aegean Sea, took some soup to Abby. The next day, we set out for Ephesus, the land of Amazons, Alexander the Great, and the Romans, and an important landmark in the history of civilization. After you walk through the entire excavated area, you can take a donkey carriage back to your car. While our carriage was passing through a tree-shaded area, I spotted this little place making *gözleme*. We could not pass the opportunity to have *ayran* and *gözleme*. That was one of the best meals we had. It cost five dollars for four people, three of us and the driver of the donkey carriage. After Ephesus and Kuşadası, we went to Pamukkale (means "cotton castle"), Bodrum, and Fethiye. Between all these destinations there were at least five or six hours of driving, and of course, no air-conditioning. In Turkey, either at gas stations or restaurants, you find these structures that are fifteen-feet high, constantly releasing cold gushing water from large pipes. It is almost like an oasis. You are supposed to drive under it and let the car have a good wash. At one place, when we stopped, Abby was so hot she just walked under the gushing water and let the water pound on her head and shoulders. She was totally wet in an instant. The owner of the place was first surprised, and later, as if he wanted to relieve us of any embarrassment, walked under the water himself. And one by one, all the people in the restaurant joined us. It took twenty minutes in the car, hot air blowing in from the windows, to be totally dry, but wrinkly when we reached our next destination, Bodrum.

Our stay in Bodrum was spectacular. We stayed at the Antique Theater Hotel, overlooking all of Bodrum and its famous castle. It is still my favorite hotel. Each room opened to a little verandah that took you to a narrow set of steps, splitting the hotel into two sections. The hotel was built on a slope, with terraces to handle five or six levels. There were bougainvilleas and white and blue jasmine everywhere.

I called you every day to see how you were doing. You were still traveling with your dad and were at Manisa visiting your Babaanne. You really wanted to be with us. I was feeling terrible not having you with us.

When we were in Fethiye, you asked me to pick you up. You said you missed me a lot. You were very sad on the phone. I could not bear to hear you crying on the phone and not be with you. For a nine-year-old, you should have been having fun and not missing your mom like that. I took an overnight bus to İzmir. Your dad was going to bring you to the bus stop. I still had another hour to wait and I knew Manisa was only thirty minutes away. I could not wait at the bus station. I took a taxi. I called your Babaanne's house and told them I was coming to pick you up. I kept the taxi running downstairs. You were so excited to see me. We took the taxi back to the İzmir bus station. The taxi driver offered to drive us all the way to Fethiye for a reasonable sum, but I would not even think about it. He did not have an air conditioner in the car, and it was almost noontime. We took a nice air-conditioned bus back to Fethiye, and you hugged me all the way there. You ended up falling asleep in my arms. You were my little angel, and you still are. Your hug was my prize for a twenty-four-hour ordeal in the heat and dust. When we arrived at the resort, we rushed to the room, got our bathing suits, and plunged into the blue sea. I finally felt complete with you being with us.

After Fethiye, we took the mountain road to Antalya. It was so serene, so beautiful—and also cooler. The Taurus Mountains and nomads created a totally different scene, almost like another country, another time in history. We ate *gözleme* again at a family road stand. We arrived just in time to return the car to the Antalya airport and waited for Nick's plane to land. He came about a week after us. A van took us to the boat that we would be taking for the Blue Voyage, from Kemer to Kaş and back to Kemer. One whole week on the Mediterranean coastline. That is what the Blue Voyage is about. You embark on a wooden yacht specific to the region. You sail on the coastline from one cove to another, one village to another. These stopping points vary. It could be Cleopatra's Beach, or Phaselis where the famous aqueducts were built in 700 B.C., or Mount Chimera where the eternal flames light up the sky at night (you can even cook tea on one of the openings emitting flames!), or an ancient Lycian city, or a tiny fishermen's village where you can buy homemade bread and pick grapes from the vines while goats are following you.

We slept on the deck on sun mattresses and cushions, watching a million stars. There were no towns, no houses, and no lights in the little harbors where we docked overnight. That made the stars shine a thousand times better. When there was a full moon, everything was lit up with moonlight. And the reflection of the moon on the water was just another point of reflection on how beautiful life is. When there was no moon, then the phosphorescence would take its place. Tiny creatures in the sea would light up with a slight movement in the water. One night, when there was no moon, we jumped into the sea and started making angels in the sea. Our arms and the water we were treading looked like they were covered with stars, all sparkling. There are no words to tell how it feels and looks when you are in water surrounded with these little creatures that sparkle with every tiny bit of motion.

We would wake up to the sunrise. I love waking up just before the sunrise, where the sea and the sky, in unison, slowly turn from dark, mysterious, and unknown to soft gray together as if they are caressing the morning. Their colors are the same and make you feel you are part of the horizon, and all the other boats in the distance look like they were hanging in the sky. I love feeling part of the soft morning. I love swimming at this time of the day with no ripple on the sea yet. While we were swimming, the captain and the cook would make breakfast for us. A bit more swimming after breakfast, and then we would go to another magnificent spot. Either a historic site or a natural beauty. It did not matter which. We would eat lunch at another place, and then either sail or motor to another beautiful spot where we would dock for our overnight stay. Another night with a million stars. We had a great time. Our fellow passengers were from Germany, Belgium, Turkey, and Italy. Every night, we would have an impromptu party with good food, good wine, and dancing, especially belly dancing.

We were all upset when the Blue Voyage ended. But, we still had a lot to see. We flew from Antalya to Ankara to see my brother and sister. My sister had already met Al during Christmas time when she was visiting us. My brother would meet Al for the first time. We spent a day in Ankara, and then Tolga drove us to Cappadocia, the land of fairy chimneys, so different than anything I had ever seen. The churches were carved into the rocks. These rocks were called *tufa*. You could carve *tufa* with a spoon and build homes in the rocks. There are hotels in Cappadocia completely carved into the rocks. We took a tour of a Hitite city, built underground. There were seven layers underground, and they had excavated only up to five layers. After returning to Ankara, Al, Nick, and Abby took a flight to İstanbul. Bora and I took a bus the same night to Çınarcık to see my parents. Now it was my mom's time. I was so excited to see her.

This was our first trip as a new integrated family. It was wonderful. In the years to follow, we took many more trips together.

Marriage Proposal

It was May 25, 1998, the second anniversary of our unforgettable date in New York. We went to the Raven and the Peach restaurant in Fair Haven, New Jersey. I should have guessed with the choice of the restaurant, but I was clueless. Again, as we always did, Al and I talked, and talked, and talked. We still talk about everything. I still enjoy every minute with him after the ten years we have been together.

That night was special. We were celebrating a great two years together, the wine was spectacular, and the food was amazing. Just at the time we finished our desserts and coffee, but still had some sips of our wine left, Al started a whole different conversation. Out of all the things he said, the only thing I remember is him saying, "I am ready to dive."

All I thought was that Al was diving into a pool with no water, marrying a hyper woman with a very active son. He was done with his kids' teenage years; he was really committing himself to go through your teenage years together with me. That meant a lot! That was really the biggest proof of how much he loved me. And he kept his promise; he really dove into our lives. He never acted as a stranger, he was never pushy, and he was not forcing any rules. The biggest thing he gave you and me is his love, his calmness, his great listening ability, and his great psychoanalytic ability. Well, he has a Ph.D. in Psychology from Brown after all. He gained your trust and love smoothly. I have never seen any moment since he moved into our home in 1999 that you and he had a big quarrel. He was the one who wrestled with you. He was the one who taught you how to be smart with words and how to respond in certain situations. He was the one who taught you how to turn the knees of the Land O'Lakes lady on the butter carton into boobs. There are never enough words to express my feelings for him just for loving me and loving you.

My life with Al is like sipping the best drink. I feel every drop, every ingredient in the drop. The glass is soft, translucent. The air is lemonade. My skin feels like I am in the Mediterranean. He is my soulmate. I found my soulmate.

So my answer was not "Do what?" It was, "Yes, yes, yes!" We left the restaurant flying. I don't think I walked that evening. I was floating with happiness. It still gives me goose bumps to think about it. We went to his apartment. Abby was staying there during the summer. The minute we told her, she jumped up and screamed. I knew then that this family would do just fine together.

You don't know yet, but hopefully you will find out. Women go crazy after the marriage proposal. There are so many things to think about: where to marry, what to wear, cake, guests, flowers, invitations, guest favors, and finally honeymoon. I ended up spending hours at Barnes and Noble looking at books. I purchased all those bridal magazines.

I just have to tell you our engagement ring story. Al did not have a ring for me. He knew that I would not choose a conventional one since I don't like removing my ring during cooking and washing. A traditional ring would bother me when I do my daily chores. It had to be a very practical ring. For that I wanted an engagement ring that does not get in the way, I could wear it all the time, and would never have to take off. It took me a month. In the meantime, Al bought me a ten dollar silver ring. I saw the picture of the wedding ring I wanted in one of the bridal magazines. The ad was from A. Jaffe, a designer from Germany. I called them and they said there were only two stores in the United States that sold the ring and one was in New York, in the diamond district, of course. One of my friends asked her mom to give us advice. Her mom had just retired as a diamond trader. We called the person she suggested and got an appointment. He was a wholesaler. After going through a few security checkpoints, we finally entered his office. I had never seen that many diamonds in my life. We finally chose a really small one. The diamond trader handed Al a little folded up paper with our diamond in it. I think the diamond burned Al's pocket until we reached the store that sells the A. Jaffe rings. They had my ring. All they had to do was to replace the cubic zirconium with our little precious diamond. The store was in one of those little malls where many merchants are side by side. They sent our diamond and the ring to the back room. Al and I followed the diamond with our eyes to ensure that it did not get stolen. As if they cared; they were dealing with diamonds five times the size of mine. But mine was special, it was from Al. I still cherish my ring. Every time I look at it, I remember the day of "ring making" and how excited I was when I put the ring on my finger and watched it sparkle. We women are sometimes suckers for such things. Think about me. I never do make up. Thanks to my curly hair, I never comb my hair. The only beauty products I buy are a facial cream and a hair conditioner for my curls. I don't dress up fancy. But I love my ring. I had so many comments from my friends about my ring. Even my neighbor, after seeing my ring, asked her father, who was an executive in Tiffany's diamond department, to replicate my ring. In platinum, of course.

Our Wedding

We looked at many typical wedding venues, but were getting disappointed. None of them made me go "Wow!" I wanted something near the water, but not in a typical wedding style. Finally we found a restaurant on the Navesink River in Rumson, the Salt Creek Grille. Downstairs there was a big meeting room that could hold a maximum of 120 people. The room had one side that was all glass, with sliding doors opening to a beautiful green rolling lawn all the way to the river. There was a narrow boat dock and a spectacular bridge spanning the river. It was the perfect setting. The restaurant manager said they had never done weddings there, just office parties. But they said they could manage. It was going to be a July wedding.

While the preparations for the wedding were moving along, Al was already living in our house. Abby was back for the summer from McGill University in Montreal. Nick just graduated in May 1999, and he had no place to stay. We invited him to stay with us. He said the only condition he had was to have his girlfriend Holly (now his wife) come and live with us too. So, here I am, a bride-to-be, getting ready for my wedding while working full time, with six people in the house. My brother and his wife came a week before the wedding. We were pretty crowded. Somehow we managed to all dress up and go to the wedding. My brother drove the car. I sat next to him. Özden, his wife, and Bora were in the back. I had a long beautiful white dress with fresh white flowers in my hair. My heart was pounding with happiness.

The wedding took place outside on the grass. All the chairs from the tables inside were arranged in a theatre seating. One of our friends' husband was a minister and officiated at the ceremony. All the attendees told me later that the people on the second floor of the restaurant were all glued to the windows, watching us. During the ceremony, I got the giggles. You know how Turkish people cannot differentiate between "w" and "v" sounds. So, I could not say my "vow." I knew I could not say it. And when the big moment came to say it, I got the giggles. Tears were coming from my eyes. I could not stop laughing. We managed to complete the ceremony, with me saying my "wow!" The song that I chose for walking down the aisle was "Gülnihal," a very old waltz from Ottoman times. Two of our friends played the music during our walk down the aisle and again after the ceremony ended. The ending music was "Telli Turnam," a great Turkish folk song.

While everyone was having drinks and chatting, all the chairs from outside were rushed inside and placed around the tables. We had exactly 120 people. Our musician was Nedim. He was a dear friend, a Turkish musician who knew how to entertain people very well. He always played at the Turkish New Year balls. That was where we met him. At one point during the wedding, I looked and there was not a single person sitting at the tables. Everybody was dancing—our American, Turkish, Israeli, Indonesian, Japanese, Brazilian, and Italian friends. And all were trying to be great belly dancers. Our wedding cake was made by my Brazilian friend's relative. It was a chocolate cake with white whipped cream frosting and decorated with swirly large pieces of coconut shavings dipped in chocolate on one side. The wedding lasted for over four hours. By the time everyone left, it was one in the morning. Al and I paid the balance of the reception cost to the hostess and walked out to our new life. A great new life.

12

When a Person Becomes a Parent

By the time this book is finished you will be in college or beyond. I am probably more anxious about it than you are. I keep my hopes high that you will do just fine. You may have a lot of clothes piled up in your dorm room, and a lot of coffee cups on your desk, but you will figure out what to do. I assume this is something that happens to many kids while they are growing up and starting their own life. But you should know that this is also a cultural difference. In Turkey, kids usually try to go to a university close to their parents' house, and they stay with their parents during the undergraduate years since it is cheaper. My sister, my brother, and I did just that. We were together until my sister got married. This did not make us more dependent on our parents. We all are quite independent kids. I think it all lies within the relationships between the kid and the parents. I was living with my parents until I got married. Even after I was married, the last year I lived in Ankara, I used to go to my mom to have lunch when I worked at the National Productivity Center of Turkey. All changed the minute I walked onto the plane on September 9, 1981 and flew to a new life. It took me a while but I managed to survive not seeing my mother every day for three years.

When a person becomes a parent, a lot of things happen. You are no longer responsible for just your own self, but become responsible for a tiny thing that is totally dependent on you for a long time. Unfortunately, there is no "Idiot's Guide" for parenting. There are a lot of books to learn from, but whatever happens you are on your own. And you, your baby, and your relationship are unique. All the theories and studies can go down the drain if they have no way of helping you. It is the hardest job to do. And it gets harder every day. But it also gets more fulfilling every day. How does a child go from a totally dependent baby that is in your tummy, connected to you with an umbilical cord, to a totally independent human being? At what stage do you let go of some strings? At what stage do you still keep things under your control even though it causes a lot of arguments? This also depends on how your parents raised you. You can take them as a model if you believe that you had a happy and a healthy childhood, or you can completely do the opposite of what they did to raise you, or follow a path somewhere in-between. I don't remember being totally independent until I got married. All I know was I was very close to my mom, and I never shared anything about my life with my dad, for obvious reasons, of course. I chose to be very close to you. I know I have more of my dad's genes than my mom's. I am impatient. I have a quick temper. But I thought if I was very close to you, you could understand my traits and help me sort out my relationship with you. I did not want you to experience the things that I lived through. You and I talked a lot, read a lot, and spent time together a lot. You shared all your fears, happiness, and anger with me. To some extent, I did the same thing. Maybe that was a bit of a mistake. I apologize if it was.

Afterword

Goodbye and Hello

I covered the stories of my loved ones, I covered the places I have been, and I covered the many steps I have taken, the many paths I have chosen. One thing that is hard to convey is how I can keep living life's ups and downs but never get tired of it. Because I love people, because I love places, and because I love being who I am. I could have been richer, smarter, more beautiful, taller, or skinnier—no ending for what I could have been. I am a very happy person, and I do my best to be better. I need to feed my soul, and for that I only need this: I need to be with you and Al, to see and be part of the Mediterranean, to read books, to give parties for my friends, to cook for a hundred people, and to change the world, even in small steps. I hope you too will create your own list. What I believe is that your steps will be bigger than mine. You have a much bigger vision for yourself and your life. And go for it. I will always be there for you.

I will continue telling you my memories. They filled my life, and there is no way I can fit them all here. Every moment, every day meant something. And like any other person, my life was not all that rosy. One thing that I see more clearly is that my days with my mother and my grandparents played a great role in helping me cope with pain, suffering, failures, and mistakes. They gave me their love. My dad gave me his intelligence and work ethics. I learned from all of them unconditional love and respect for individuals. That is what I wanted to give you in every way possible since you were born.

I just want to finish this book with the story about our "goodbye session." Stephanie, our therapist of ten years, called and asked us to see her. She wanted to have a ninety-minute session with us before your departure for Cornell. She was my mother earth, my friend, and support when I felt I was down in the deep trenches. Well, she was really a great "paid" friend for ten years. She wanted to see us to say goodbye to each other.

She does sand art therapy in addition to her ability to read you inside and out. She asked each of us to pick two objects representing what we think describes the best about the other. And she asked us to pick three objects that represent the three traits that we want the other to change. We were not supposed to talk to each other during our selections. In the middle of my selections for the three "change" traits for Bora, I asked Stephanie if I could choose one more. A few minutes later, Bora asked the same thing. And Stephanie said "Like mother, like son. They can change rules if that helps them."

For "positive traits" I chose a pure crystal ball to represent the pureness of your heart. I also chose a young successful male figure to represent your goals and ambitions and my belief that you will succeed. Or, were they my goals and ambitions about you? You chose a lion and a comfortable chair. The lion was for my pride, my achievements, and how proud you are of me, my strength, and what made me come this far. The chair was, as you said it, "No matter what happens to me, I can go to my mom. She is my comfort, she is my chair. I will find relief talking to her and being with her."

Of course the negative objects were not that pleasing, but they meant a lot. You chose a whirling dervish to represent Turkish culture. Although I tried hard to remember that we were living in the United States, not in Turkey, and I was very careful to adapt as a mother of a child born in the United States and growing up with kids born here, I still was holding onto my traditions of raising a kid with some Turkish values. You thought I was after you too much, taking care of you, checking where you were, what you ate, what you wore in cold weather, and whether you had done your homework or not. I apologize if I bugged you a lot. I did my best to let you breathe more, especially after Al came into our lives. He was a great influence on you and was a great balancing factor. However, one thing I look back and feel great about was that you never cursed at me. You were angry at me once in a while, but you were never disrespectful. You always cared about your family. The other objects you chose were mostly around the same issue.

And the day came. You were leaving for college. We drove to Ithaca on August 16. The car was packed with your belongings and new items for your new life at Cornell. We were doing what any college bound family was doing—driving a car full of college stuff to your new life. You stayed with us at Abby's house (she was at Cornell attending graduate school) for two days, and on Friday August 18 at 10:30 a.m. we drove to your dorm, Clara Dickson Hall, Room 5692. You shooed us out, rightfully, after your room looked good and most things were in place, except for a few boxes. We had dinner together that night and drove you back to your new room, where you would be spending the first college night. The next day, you did not even want to come with us to dinner, you were already doing what you were supposed to do: socializing.

Al bought me a book to read on the way back home, titled *Don't Tell Me What to Do, Just Send Money*. As I read the pages, my tears turned into laughter as I realized I was not the only one going through this. I am a mom who is very proud to see her kid go to college. I am a mom who loves her kid. I am a mom who will learn to let go and live her life with a kid in college. I will miss you a lot, and I will see you a lot. Things will be different, but never my love for you. I am me, I am your mom.

Though I said goodbye, this is also a hello from me to you, welcoming you to your new life. I am here for you as your comforting chair.

"To overcome lies in the heart, in the streets, in the books from the lullabies of the mothers to the news report that the speaker reads, understanding, my love, what a great joy it is, to understand what is gone and what is on the way."

Nazım Hikmet (1902-1963)